EYEWITNESS
AMERICAN REVOLUTION

Signaling horn

Tea chest

British
regimental
coat

Poster by Paul Revere

Snuff box

Smoothbore
musket

Drum

American artillerymen
loading a cannon

Continental
money

SMITHSONIAN

EYEWITNESS

AMERICAN
REVOLUTION

WRITTEN BY
STUART MURRAY

Telescope

Candle
lantern

Woman's dress

REVISED EDITION

DK LONDON

Senior Editor Carron Brown **Senior Art Editor** Lynne Moulding
US Senior Editor Kayla Dugger **US Executive Editor** Lori Cates Hand
Managing Editor Francesca Baines
Managing Art Editor Philip Letsu
Production Editor Gillian Reid
Production Controller Sian Cheung
Senior Jackets Designer Surabhi Wadhwa-Gandhi
Jacket Design Development Manager Sophia MTT
Publisher Andrew Macintyre
Associate Publishing Director Liz Wheeler
Art Director Karen Self
Publishing Director Jonathan Metcalf

Consultant Philip Baselice

DK DELHI

Senior Editor Shatarupa Chaudhuri **Senior Art Editor** Vikas Chauhan
Project Art Editor Heena Sharma
Editor Sai Prasanna
Project Picture Researcher Aditya Katyal
Managing Editor Kingshuk Ghoshal **Managing Art Editor** Govind Mittal
Senior DTP Designer Jagtar Singh
DTP Designers Pawan Kumar, Mohd Rizwan, Rakesh Kumar
Jacket Designer Juhi Sheth

FIRST EDITION

MEDIA PROJECTS INC.

Executive Editor C. Carter Smith **Managing Editor** Carter Smith
Project Editor Aaron Murray **Designer** Laura Smyth
Photo Researchers Robyn Bissette (S.I.), Athena Angelos

DK LONDON

Editors Beth Sutinis, Elizabeth Hester, Carter Smith
Senior Art Editor Michelle Baxter
Creative Director Tina Vaughan **Jacket Art Director** Dirk Kaufman
Publisher Andrew Berkhut **Production Manager** Chris Avgherinos

This Eyewitness ® Book has been conceived by
Dorling Kindersley Limited and Editions Gallimard

This American Edition, 2022
First American Edition, 2002
Published in the United States by DK Publishing
1450 Broadway, Suite 801, New York, NY 10018

Library of Congress Cataloging-in-Publication Data
Murray, Stuart, 1948-American Revolution/by Stuart Murray.
American Revolution.—1st American ed.
p. cm.–(Dorling Kindersley eyewitness books)
Written in association with the Smithsonian Institution.
Summary: A visual guide, accompanied by text, to the people,
battles, and events of America's war for independence.

1. United States—History—Revolution, 1775-1783—Juvenile literature.
[1. United States—History—Revolution, 1775-1783.] I. Dorling
Kindersley Publishing, Inc. II. Smithsonian Institution. III. Series.
E208 .A427 2002
973.3—dc21
2001047619

ISBN 978-0-7440-5226-8 (Paperback)
ISBN 978-0-7440-5227-5 (ALB)

DK books are available at special discounts when purchased in bulk
for sales promotions, premiums, fund-raising, or educational use.
For details, contact: DK Publishing Special Markets,
1450 Broadway, Suite 801, New York, NY 10018
SpecialSales@dk.com

Printed and bound in China

For the curious
www.dk.com

Smithsonian

Established in 1846, the Smithsonian is
the world's largest museum and research complex,
dedicated to public education, national service,
and scholarship in the arts, sciences, and history. It
includes 19 museums and galleries and the National
Zoological Park. The total number of artifacts,
works of art, and specimens in the Smithsonian's
collection is estimated at 155.5 million.

MIX
Paper from
responsible sources
FSC™ C018179

This book was made with Forest
Stewardship Council™ certified
paper—one small step in DK's
commitment to a sustainable future.
For more information go to www.dk.
com/our-green-pledge

Ethan Allen's
compass

Liberty Cap
weather vane

Badge of
Military Merit

Pipe tomahawk

Rhode Island
infantryman

Regimental flag

Contents

George Washington's
sword and scabbard

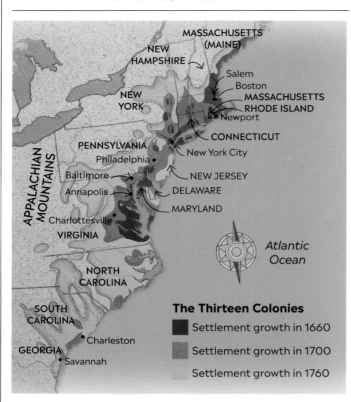

The American colonies that rose up against British rule lay along the Atlantic seaboard. European and African populations are shown for 1660 (dark green), 1700 (lighter green), and 1760 (lightest green).

The Thirteen Colonies
- Settlement growth in 1660
- Settlement growth in 1700
- Settlement growth in 1760

British America

After the Seven Years' War in the British American colonies ended in 1763, peace and prosperity came to the Thirteen Colonies. By 1775, there were more than 2,700,000 colonists, and Philadelphia was a leading city in the British Empire. The ports of New York, Boston, and Charleston were booming. Each colony elected its own lawmaking assembly and had its own governor, although most were appointed by the king. At peace with France and in possession of Canada after the war, the British government intended to keep the American colonies under strict control.

New England

The four New England colonies of Rhode Island, Massachusetts, Connecticut, and New Hampshire relied on fishing, farming, shipbuilding, and seafaring. The unsettled region of Maine contained great trees to build ship masts. New England had many free laborers, as well as skilled artisans, such as carpenters and goldsmiths. There were few slaves.

Freedom suit
Young men often worked for a tradesman as indentured servants by signing a contract for seven years to learn a skill. They got some amenities but no salary. At the end, they might receive a "freedom suit," such as this one from Rhode Island.

A captain's diary
Captain Ashley Bowen of Marblehead, Massachusetts, recorded his voyages and drew pictures of ships in his diary (as shown here). As part of the Siege of Quebec, 1759, he wrote, "We were in Rear Admiral Durell Division and sailed for Quebec May the 3 ..."

The colonial kitchen
A colonial family in Malden, Massachusetts, gathered here for meals and prayers, or sat by the hearth to do handiwork or repair tools.

The Middle Colonies

New York, New Jersey, Pennsylvania, and Delaware each had two large cities. Philadelphia was bustling with trade and commerce and was rich in colonial culture, such as music and art. New York was one of the busiest ports in the empire, and it was also a center of trade with Indigenous peoples.

A New Jersey eighteen pence banknote, issued in 1776

The State House
The colonial government of Pennsylvania met in Philadelphia at the State House, built in 1732–1741.

Quaker farm
This prosperous 18th-century Pennsylvania farm shows a bustling summertime scene, with the family and hired hands plowing fields and managing horses and other livestock. In 1775, most colonists lived on farms.

Slave quarters
Africans who were first brought to Virginia in 1619 were enslaved as field laborers. Enslaved families on large Southern plantations sometimes lived in cabins, but they were often crowded together in large barracks where there was little privacy.

The Southern Colonies

Most white people in Maryland, Virginia, North Carolina, South Carolina, and Georgia lived on family farms, but large-scale plantations dominated the economic and social systems. To produce cash crops—mainly tobacco, indigo, and rice—for markets, the plantations relied on enslaved labor. People were brought to America, mainly from West Africa, and then enslaved and forced to work without pay against their will.

Virginia's capital
Virginia's capital, Williamsburg, boasted its own magnificent government building. The House of Burgesses in Virginia was the first elected "representative" legislature in the American colonies.

War in the New World

Whenever France and England were at war, their American colonies also fought. The great Seven Years' War, which started in 1754, saw the two mighty empires clash on land and at sea. The French won major battles early on. Eventually, the British colonists and Redcoat soldiers outnumbered their foe and became too strong for the French, causing French strongholds, such as Quebec, to become British territories. With the coming of peace, there would still be local conflicts, but the American colonies were strong as never before.

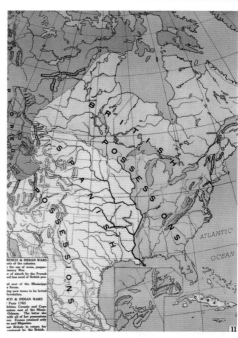

Victory in the Seven Years' War broke French power in America, bringing vast areas of eastern North America into the British Empire, as shown on this map.

Washington

Troops from Virginia were led by George Washington. While traveling through western Pennsylvania and the Ohio Valley, he wrote many reports for headquarters. At the age of 26, he was the only American-born officer to command a British brigade during the war.

George Washington, c. 1772

Grand strategist

British prime minister William Pitt planned campaigns to capture French Canada.

Braddock's road

In July 1755, the arrogant British general Edward Braddock led an army of 1,400 soldiers against the French and Indigenous Americans defending Fort Duquesne. His army was ambushed; however, a young George Washington organized the retreat of the survivors. There were around 1,000 British-led casualties, including Braddock, who was buried under the road that was given his name.

Enduring mementos
Hundreds of British and French cannonballs littered the battlefields of this war. These were found at Fort Ticonderoga, a French-built bastion on Lake Champlain.

French cannonball with royal fleur-de-lis symbol

"King's Arrow," also called "Broad Arrow," shows cannonball is royal property

Regimental coat
Major John Dagworthy, an officer in the 44th Regiment of Foot, wore this coat. He fought in the Seven Years' War.

Pontiac's Rebellion
After the war, some Indigenous peoples who had fought with the defeated French refused to accept British rule. Led by Ottawa chief Pontiac, several nations attacked British garrisons in May 1763 and laid siege to Fort Detroit. Warriors also drove out thousands of settlers. This forced the British to recognize land rights for Indigenous Americans. A British proclamation declared the lands from the Appalachians to the Mississippi River from Florida to Quebec as Indigenous land where colonists were forbidden to trespass.

Fall of Quebec
The last great French stronghold in Canada, Quebec City stood high above the Saint Lawrence River. In September 1759, General James Wolfe and his British troops rowed to an undefended cliff track, defeating the French, who were led by the Marquis de Montcalm. Both commanders died in battle.

Return of prisoners
In Pontiac's Rebellion, warriors rose up against the British and took prisoners. But upon defeat, chiefs of the Shawnee and Delaware nations met with British commander Colonel Henry Bouquet to arrange for the return of settlers.

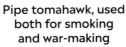

Pipe tomahawk, used both for smoking and war-making

Taxation without representation

In the 1760s, the British Parliament created acts that forced the colonies to pay tax on imports, such as sugar and tea. Since colonies did not elect representatives to Parliament, many Americans proclaimed that "taxation without representation" was illegal. Angry colonists refused to import British goods until the acts were lifted. In 1768, 4,000 Redcoats occupied Boston to punish the city for its resistance. Then in 1770, they fired on a rowdy mob—this is called the "Boston Massacre."

"No Stamp Act"

A Virginia family's teapot makes clear their opposition to the 1765 Stamp Act requiring legal documents to have revenue stamps. Such stamps were kept in this leather box.

"GR" stands for "George Rex," or King George

Tax collector's box

1766 Williamsburg teapot

Embossed official stamps could be impressed upon paper

Revenue stamps

Tarred and feathered
Radical Bostonians attack a tax collector, coating him with hot tar and covering him with feathers.

Samuel Adams
One of the most outspoken opponents of Parliament's taxation policies, Samuel Adams was also among the first people to consider separation from Britain.

The Boston Massacre

In 1770, British soldiers were harassed by a threatening mob. Some angry Redcoats fired, killing five people. Put on trial, the soldiers were defended by attorney John Adams, who won acquittals for most, and only light punishment for others. Although an advocate of American independence, Adams showed he was fair and impartial as he defended the British soldiers in court.

Fiery propaganda
A poster by engraver Paul Revere depicts troops at the Boston Massacre firing together on command, which was not the case.

Boston Tea Party
Several ships carrying imported tea were attacked by colonial protesters. On December 16, 1773, locals disguised as Indigenous Americans threw 342 tea chests into Boston Harbor to protest the 1773 Tea Act. It was organized by Patriot leader Samuel Adams, who founded the resistance group Sons of Liberty, whose motto was "No taxation without representation."

Tea chest
This is a miniature replica of one of the East Indian tea boxes said to have been thrown into Boston Harbor.

Opposing leaders

Supported by King George III, Prime Minister Lord North led military efforts to bring the colonies under control. Some British statesmen and generals, however, were against armed conflict. George Washington from Virginia was chosen to be commander in chief of the Continental Army. New England Patriots John Adams, a lawyer and political theorist, and John Hancock, a wealthy merchant, were among the first delegates to the Continental Congress.

Emblem of royalty
The British royal coat of arm includes the symbols o England, Scotland, Wales and Ireland

Lord Frederick North
Prime Minister Lord North supported the tax on the colonies. He allied himself with King George and opposed men like the statesman Edmund Burke, who objected to Britain's colonial policies.

Sir William Howe
Spending most of his career in America, General Howe did not agree with British colonial policies. Yet from 1775, he led the British army in North America.

Image of Howe published in 1777

Royal proclamation
In 1775, King George's royal proclamation declared the American colonies to be in rebellion. Many colonists, he said, had forgotten the allegiance "they owe to the power that has protected and supported them."

The British sovereign
Shown here in regal attire, King George III was just 22 when he took the throne in 1760 Americans petitioned the king to support the colonies' position, but he refused

The American commander in chief

The Second Continental Congress appointed George Washington commander of all its forces because of his military experience. Washington believed the military must never take the reins of power in a republic. He also refused to become directly involved in politics while he was a soldier.

owel

Strap

Leader's spurs

In the winter of 1777–1778, Washington's hungry army at Valley Forge, Pennsylvania, needed food and clothing. He gave his own spurs to an officer who wore them on a ride of more than 300 miles to Boston to arrange for supplies.

At home in Virginia
Washington's powerful physique combined with his wisdom and courage helped him endure eight years as commander in chief. He is pictured at his beloved Mount Vernon plantation in Virginia. He left home at the start of the Revolution and did not return for six years.

The first signer

Evading British capture for not paying port fees, Boston patriot John Hancock later became the president of the first and Second Continental Congresses. He was the first person to sign the Declaration of Independence.

John Jay

A brilliant New York attorney and jurist, Jay was a delegate to the Continental Congress and, later, an important diplomat. He was president of Congress from 1778–1779.

A political mastermind

Lawyer John Adams of Massachusetts was an early challenger to British colonial policy. After helping draft the Declaration of Independence, Adams served in France as representative for the United States.

A Briton for America

Edmund Burke called—unsuccessfully—for the British Parliament to negotiate peacefully with the American colonies. He also championed the rights of other British colonies, including India.

👁 EYEWITNESS

Defending liberty
Lawyer James Otis Jr. (1725–1783) was one of the first Americans to openly oppose slavery. He wrote, "The colonists are by the law of nature freeborn, as indeed all men are, white or black." He called slavery "the most shocking violation of the law of nature."

Patrick Henry
A radical Virginia legislator, Henry believed King George had no right to rule America. He famously said, "Give me liberty or give me death!"

Revolution
in the air

After the Boston Tea Party, Parliament voted in 1774 to place harsh regulations—called "Intolerable Acts" or "Coercive Acts"—on the colony of Massachusetts. Set up in Philadelphia, the First Continental Congress united the colonies to stop buying British goods until Parliament repealed their laws. Americans made goods at home to replace British imports, and a Second Continental Congress was planned for 1775 if Britain did not change its policies.

Raleigh Tavern's signboard

The Raleigh Tavern

In 1774, Virginia legislators met at Raleigh Tavern, named after the English adventurer Sir Walter Raleigh—misspelled "Ralegh" on its signboard. They agreed to boycott British goods, arm the colony, and send delegates to the First Continental Congress in Philadelphia.

Pewter ware
Many colonial tavern items, from plates to mugs, were made of pewter—tin combined with lead, antimony, or copper.

Snuff box made of pewter

Drinking mug, or "tankard"

Preparing for conflict

The colonies armed to resist British oppression, and gunsmiths turned out muskets as fast as they could. These were called "flintlocks," because pulling the trigger caused a flint to strike a spark and fire the musket ball. By early 1775, many Americans were ready to fight for colonial freedom.

Musket flints

Paper cartridge holds a musket ball and gunpowder

Manufacturing muskets
American gunsmiths were skilled at making long-barreled hunting rifles and muskets, but soldiers needed short muskets that could have a bayonet. Rapid firing and bayonet charges by massed troops were essential to the success of an 18th-century army. American-made muskets were known as "Committee of Safety Muskets."

Spinning and weaving for liberty
Defying Parliament, Patriot women mobilized to support the war effort by spinning thread and weaving cloth to replace fabric normally imported from the British Empire. They held "spinning bees"—public events where women gathered to make clothing for colonists. These "Daughters of Liberty" worked to make the colonies more self-sufficient.

Multitalented statesman

Benjamin Franklin was a Philadelphia author, publisher, and scientist. Early on, he worked as a printer in England. He later returned to London as a colonial representative. In 1775, after an unsuccessful negotiation between Parliament and the colonists, he came back to America, expecting an armed struggle.

Portrait of Franklin

The Gadsden Flag
In 1775, Patriot and Lieutenant Governor of South Carolina Christopher Gadsden designed the Gadsden Flag by adapting Franklin's idea. It was used by the Continental Marines as a symbol of resistance.

"Join, or die"
Franklin's sketch, published in 1754, shows the individual American colonies as a snake cut into pieces. For the snake—and the colonies—to survive, the parts must unite to work together.

JOIN, or DIE.

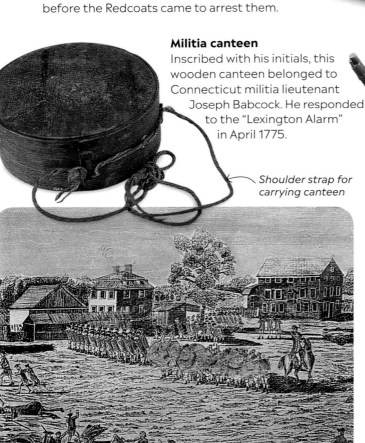

The Revolution begins

On April 18, 1775, General Thomas Gage ordered Redcoats to look for stockpiles of colonial military supplies in Concord. Patriot leader Dr. Joseph Warren sent out riders to alert the militia. The next day—and after much shooting—the militia forced the marching Redcoats to retreat. The Americans laid siege to Boston, and the Revolution began.

"One if by land, two if by sea"
This is one of two candle lanterns placed in Boston's Old North Church's spire on the night of April 18, 1775. Two lanterns meant that Redcoats were crossing to the mainland by boat, not land.

The ride of Paul Revere
Revere alerted leaders John Hancock and Samuel Adams in Lexington of British plans. They escaped before the Redcoats came to arrest them.

Militia canteen
Inscribed with his initials, this wooden canteen belonged to Connecticut militia lieutenant Joseph Babcock. He responded to the "Lexington Alarm" in April 1775.

Shoulder strap for carrying canteen

Statue cast in bronze

The Minuteman
This statue honors the Massachusetts militiamen of 1775, who left their plows to fight against Redcoats marching out of Boston.

Lexington Green
British major John Pitcairn shouted "Disperse, ye rebels!" at defiant Minutemen gathered on Lexington Green, and a moment later firing broke out.

A bloody retreat

After reaching Concord, the Redcoats found themselves surrounded by thousands of armed militia. The march back to Boston 20 miles (32 km) away became a fierce, running battle all through the day.

Engraved silver decoration

Pitcairn's pistols
Under heavy rebel fire during the Redcoat retreat to Boston, Major Pitcairn's horse bolted, carrying away his pistols. They were captured by the militia.

Capture of Fort Ticonderoga

The once-mighty "Fort Ti" was in poor repair in 1775 and was occupied by only a few British soldiers, but it controlled strategic Lake Champlain. On May 10, Ethan Allen and Benedict Arnold attacked the fort with their rebel group. The British commander, Captain William Delaplace, was ordered to surrender or die—he surrendered.

Allen's compass
Ethan Allen used his sundial compass to reach "Fort Ti." A broadside (below) announced the fort's capture in New York and New England.

British commander, Captain William Delaplace

Ethan Allen demands the surrender of Fort Ticonderoga.

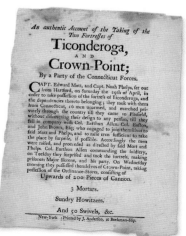

Printed broadside (poster) announces taking of Fort Ticonderoga

Breed's Hill
and Boston

On June 16, 1775, hundreds of American militiamen dug fortifications on Breed's Hill, on the Charlestown peninsula, across the Charles River from Boston. The orders were to take nearby Bunker Hill, but rebel general Israel Putnam mistakenly seized Breed's Hill. General Gage's Redcoat regiments attacked and were pushed back twice before they won. The British suffered around 1,000 casualties—the highest loss during the entire war. The battle was critical for the American militia, as it proved they could take on the British military. General George Washington arrived two weeks later to take command of the siege.

Charlestown burns
British artillery in Boston and on warships fired red-hot cannonballs into Charlestown, setting it ablaze.

Prescott calms his men
The British fired cannonballs into the entrenchments on Breed's Hill. When a man was killed, Colonel William Prescott leaped into the open, defying the fire.

Thomas Gage
General Gage was commander of British troops in the colonies. He had tried to avoid bloodshed, but after Lexington and Concord his army was trapped in Boston by thousands of angry rebels.

Breed's Hill attack
The Redcoats finally defeated the Americans with their third assault. Among the American dead was Dr. Joseph Warren; among the British was Major Pitcairn of the Royal Marines, fatally wounded by Black soldier Peter Salem.

British ships

Washington reviews his troops

General George Washington took command of the rebel army, besieging Boston and soon building strong defenses to prevent the British from attacking.

Silver lion head pommel

Ivory grip

Putnam's sword

Patriot general Israel Putnam, a leader at the siege of Boston, owned this sword. It could have served as a weapon for combat or as a dress sword for formal occasions.

Opening 8 in (20 cm) wide

"In Defence of Liberty" is carved into horn

Bronze mortar barrel weighs 700 lb (318 kg)

Steel blade, 27 in (68 cm) long

Powder horn

Soldiers kept gunpowder in hollowed-out horns of cow, ox, or buffalo, which they often decorated with carved pictures. This horn was carried by Connecticut soldier Frederick Robbins during the siege of Boston.

Rebel guns come to Boston

In the winter of 1775-1776, Henry Knox and his men carted 59 heavy guns to Boston from captured Fort Ticonderoga. It included mortars like this one, which could fire explosive shells high into the air and drop them onto a target. Washington fortified Dorchester Heights and positioned the cannon where the British could not hit them, forcing them to eventually surrender.

The British evacuate Boston

Before leaving, Howe's men destroyed what military supplies they could not take and threw some heavy cannon into the bay to prevent the Americans from getting them.

Recruiting
and training

In 1775, many Americans were members of militia companies—mainly social clubs that met a couple of times a year on "training days." When the Revolution started, men turned out with local militia for a short term of service. The states and Congress soon formed regiments that enlisted men for longer terms, teaching them military basics. In time, American soldiers were able to stand up against the Redcoats and earned their respect. George Washington requested Indigenous warriors from the Oneida and Tuscarora tribes to join the Continental Army to serve as scouts. They joined him at Valley Forge in 1778.

The drummer
A company's drummer rapped out beats to prompt men to get up, to eat, and more. In battle, drum beats helped officers move their troops.

First recruits for the Revolution
Officers taught unskilled volunteers how to handle muskets. By 1779, the best American regiments had uniforms and knew how to march. In later battles, these troops impressed both their French allies and British enemies.

Equipping the recruits

Militia carried their own firearms, while the regiments of the states and Congress used government-issue weapons. Congress and the states could not pay their troops, who usually suffered from few supplies. This was evident from George Washington's many letters begging Congress for equipment. Most soldiers had to make their own musket balls using musket ball molds.

Leather cartridge box for carrying ammunition

Musket ball mold

A New Jersey soldier's wallet with state money

Musket ball

HANDLING A MUSKET

As the American army developed, manuals were created to teach soldiers. This manual showed the steps for using a musket. In battle, soldiers stood in ranks, firing and reloading together on command.

Henry Knox

Before the Revolution, Henry Knox from Boston served in a militia artillery unit, learning military history and tactics from books. He then trained other officers, who created artillerymen.

A major's coat

Colonel Peter Gansevoort wore this uniform coat as commander of the 3rd New York Continental Regiment, made up of Dutch-descended soldiers from the Albany region.

Woolen jacket, colored blue with indigo dyes

Red facings

Musician's pride

This drum was used throughout the Revolution. Drums had to be cared for so they could send loud signals to the troops.

Buckskin breeches

Dragoons rode on horses to battle but usually dismounted to fight on foot. They wore buckskin breeches, which protected them from sharp branches and saddle sores.

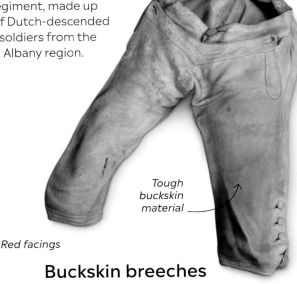

Tough buckskin material

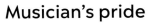

The two armies

Nicknamed "Redcoats" because of their red jackets, the British army came from England, Scotland, Ireland, and Wales. They were joined by thousands of German soldiers from Hesse-Kassel called "Hessians"—mercenary soldiers hired by the British, as well as American Loyalists. The American Revolutionary army consisted of blue- or brown-coated regiments raised by the Continental Congress and regiments belonging to the states. Continental and British infantry carried smoothbore muskets and used the same basic battle tactics: massed firing by ranks and charging with the bayonet.

Informative badge
This badge indicated a British soldier of the 26th Regiment of Foot.

British grenadier
Each regiment had men trained to throw grenades. By 1775, these men were the elite troops, distinguished by their tall hats.

The Loyalists

A third of Americans remained loyal to Britain, and thousands fought for them. British officer Banastre Tarleton created a Loyalist cavalry legion, and Scottish colonists opposed to the Revolution created the 84th Royal Highland Emigrant Regiment.

84th Royal Highland Emigrant Regiment camp flag

Tarleton's Legion cavalryman

Triumphant occupation
Redcoats and their German allies parade through New York City while mounted officers and civilians look on. The city was captured by the king's forces in the summer of 1776. It was garrisoned by Redcoats, German troops, and Loyalists throughout the rest of the war.

Philadelphia Light Horse flag

The Philadelphia Light Horse was a distinguished Revolutionary unit made up of men from leading Pennsylvania families.

Smoothbore musket

Revolutionary hat

American colonists usually wore three-corner hats called tricorns.

Standing strong

The Continental infantry man, or "line soldier," was trained to stand firmly in rank during the heat of battle.

Integrated unit

In 1778, the Rhode Island Assembly voted to allow every able-bodied male slave—whether Black, of mixed Black and white ancestry, or Indigenous—"to enlist into either of the Continental Battalions." The 1st Rhode Island Regiment consisted of Black, Indigenous American, and white soldiers.

Soldier of the Rhode Island Regiment

Drumbeat of discipline

The American army learned to march, form up in ranks, and behave like disciplined soldiers. The drum and fife set the rhythm for marching troops and sounded out battle commands and signals.

Artillery

American artillerymen were essential to Revolutionary forces. Forges from New England to Virginia made cannon and shot, but American gunners were always short of equipment. They often used guns and gear supplied by their French allies and reused British cannonballs picked up during battles.

"King's Arrow" states that cannonball is royal property

At the Siege of Boston, the Continental Army collected
700 cannonballs
that the British had fired at them.

Artillery gauge shows the angle at which the cannon barrel must be placed to hit a given target

Shell for explosive

Rebel gun crew
Before reloading, artillerymen use a damp sponge to cool the gun's muzzle and prevent sparks from flying.

Early northern battles

Late in 1775, Americans marched against the Canadian towns of Montreal and Quebec to prevent the British navy from landing a powerful force there. Led by New York generals Philip Schuyler and Richard Montgomery, the expedition captured Montreal in November and moved against Quebec. Then another expedition—commanded by Benedict Arnold of Connecticut—crossed the Maine wilderness in a brutal march to join them. But the combined American force was defeated at Quebec, and Montgomery was killed.

FIRST FIGHTS

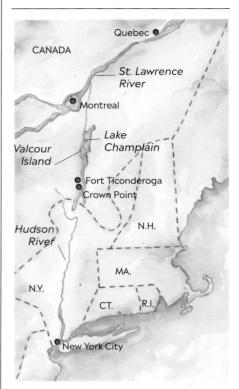

Early clashes were in the Lake Champlain-Hudson River corridor—the main travel route between Canada and New York.

Montgomery's officer's sash

Earliest trophy

The flag of the British Seventh Regiment of Foot was the first ever captured by an American force. It was won in 1775 at the surrender of Fort Chambly.

The taking of Ethan Allen

During the American campaign to capture Montreal in late 1775, the British and Canadians trapped Ethan Allen and his volunteers.

Montgomery falls

On December 31, 1775, American brigadier general Richard Montgomery was struck by cannon fire in the failed assault on Quebec. The second-in-command, Colonel Benedict Arnold, shown arriving at right, was also wounded in the defeat.

Battle of Valcour Island

In October 1776, Arnold forced the British fleet on Lake Champlain to attack his vessels at Valcour Island. Arnold's flotilla was destroyed, but its fierce resistance made the British fear the lake could not be captured before winter set in.

Up from the depths
The gunboat *Philadelphia*, sunk at Valcour Island, was raised in 1935. It is the oldest American fighting vessel in existence.

12-pounder gun in its original carriage

Gunboat is 54 ft (16 m) long

Retreat to fight again
Several American vessels escaped from the Valcour Island defeat, but most were badly damaged. Some were even set on fire, so their crews had to run them aground and flee on foot.

Independence

In June 1776, the Second Continental Congress met in Philadelphia and appointed a five-member committee to draft a document stating the reasons for separating from England. The Lee Resolution (the independence vote proposed by Richard Henry Lee) was passed on July 2. The same day, a Pennsylvania newspaper announced, "This day the Continental Congress declared the United Colonies Free and Independent States." Thomas Jefferson had composed the first draft of the declaration, which was presented to Congress and finally approved on July 4.

Jefferson's desk

Jefferson used this folding portable writing desk to draft the Declaration. After many hours of solitary thinking, he returned to his desk to compose. The drawer holds writing implements, such as quills and ink.

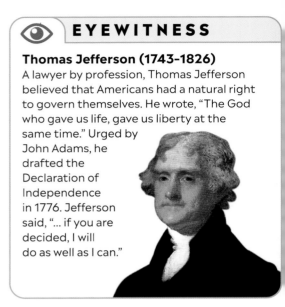

Drawer for paper, pens, and inkwell

The labor of liberty
Discarded pages litter the floor as Benjamin Franklin (left) and John Adams (center) help Jefferson (right) prepare the document.

Common sense

In 1776, the 50-page pamphlet *Common Sense* by philosopher Thomas Paine stirred up an American belief in liberty. He asserted that government was created to serve the people and foster their happiness, not oppress them. He said, "the last cord is now broken" between America and Britain.

COMMON SENSE;

ADDRESSED TO THE

INHABITANTS

OF

AMERICA,

On the following interesting

SUBJECTS.

I. Of the Origin and Design of Government in general, with concise Remarks on the English Constitution.

II. Of Monarchy and Hereditary Succession.

III. Thoughts on the present State of American Affairs.

IV. Of the present Ability of America, with some miscellaneous Reflections.

Man knows no Master save creating HEAVEN,
Or those whom choice and common good ordain.
THOMSON.

PHILADELPHIA;

Printed, and Sold, by R. BELL, in Third-Street.

MDCCLXXVI.

Presenting to Congress

On July 1, 1776, committeemen (from left to right) Adams, Roger Sherman of Connecticut, Robert Livingston of New York, Jefferson, and Franklin presented their finished document to Congress's president John Hancock, seated.

The assembly room

This chamber in Philadelphia's Independence Hall was where Congress met to approve the Declaration. Hancock was at the center rear, while delegates sat at the other tables.

> **"We hold these truths to be self evident, that all men are created equal, that they are endowed ... with certain**
> # unalienable Rights ...
> **Life, Liberty and the pursuit of Happiness."**
> **—Declaration of Independence, 1776**

Congress's inkstand

Delegates used the quills of this silver inkstand to sign the Declaration.

John Hancock's signature

The Declaration of Independence

Signed by delegates from all the states, the Declaration bore the subhead, "The unanimous Declaration of the thirteen united States of America." Although the declaration stated "all men are created equal," many of the founding fathers owned enslaved labor. Some of them supported a gradual end to slavery, but no one proposed an immediate end.

Into battle

After evacuating Boston in 1776, British general Howe sent a small expedition to Charleston, South Carolina, but it was driven back. Next, he invaded New York to defeat Washington's army, which retreated ultimately to Pennsylvania, and it seemed Philadelphia would also soon fall to the British. But on December 26, Washington defeated the Hessians at Trenton. He won the Second Battle of Trenton on January 2, 1777. On January 3, he triumphed over a British force at Princeton. The Patriot army marched to the New Jersey hills, where it would remain over winter. Washington was striking back.

Symbol of liberty
Moultrie's troops kept the Moultrie flag flying on Sullivan's Island. The flag became a symbol of liberty and of the Revolutionary cause in the South

Great defender
On Sullivan's Island, South Carolina's Colonel William Moultrie had only 21 guns against 10 enemy warships. But his men fired more accurately than the British.

A failed British attack

On June 28, 1776, British commander Sir Henry Clinton led nine warships and 2,500 Redcoats against Charleston in the Battle of Sullivan's Island. His troops tried to attack the fort on Sullivan's Island, which guarded the harbor, but they were forced back. The fort's guns pounded the warships and the invasion was called off. Charleston was saved.

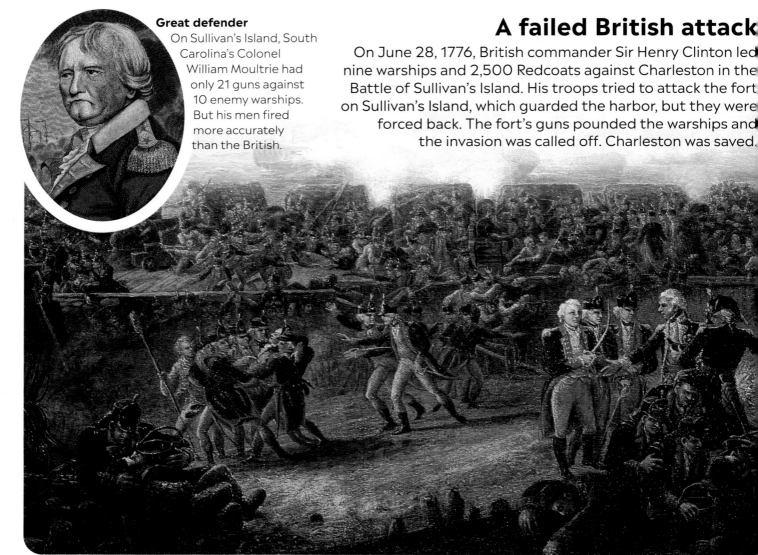

The Battle of Long Island

In August 1776, Sir William Howe sent 20,000 soldiers against Washington's 8,000-man army, which was fortified on Long Island. The Patriots were defeated and trapped against the East River, but at night Washington evacuated his army to Manhattan Island.

A second stunning blow

In January 1777, the British general Lord Cornwallis came after Washington to avenge the Trenton defeat. But Washington's 5,200-man army beat Cornwallis's soldiers at Princeton.

Lord Cornwallis

Grenadier cap

Like the British, some Patriot troops wore tall caps to show they were in an elite company called grenadiers. This cap belonged to a soldier of the 26th Continental Infantry Regiment, which fought at Trenton in 1776.

Grenade design

Bullet mold

Soldiers made ammunition using molds, such as this one carved from soapstone. Molten lead was poured into the channels and then cooled to produce musket balls.

Signal horn

Drums, whistles, fifes, bagpipes, and horns were used to send orders to troops. A signaling horn could be heard a long way over the din of battle.

Rising from defeat

Driven from New York in 1776, Washington's army retreated across the Delaware River. On the night of December 26, he crossed back over the ice-choked river and surprised the Hessians at Trenton. The victory stunned the British high command.

Washington Crossing the Delaware by Emanuel Leutze

Continued from previous page

THE COURSE OF WAR

Quebec •
Montreal •

CANADA

Maine
(part of Ma.)

Lake Champlain

Ft. Ticonderoga

N.H.

Saratoga •
Lake Ontario   Oriskany   Albany   Ma.   Lexington & Concord
                                            • Boston
New York   R.I.
                                            • Newport
Newburgh   Ct.
West Point
Stony Point
Lake Erie   Delaware R   Long Island
• Ft. Detroit   Pennsylvania   Ft. Lee   Battle of Long Island
                 Morristown   New York City (Ft. Washington)
                 Princeton   Monmouth
                 Germantown   Trenton
                 Valley Forge   Philadelphia
                                Brandywine

Md.   De.

Virginia

Williamsburg • • Yorktown

Allegheny Mountains

Chesapeake Bay

Hudson River

St. Lawrence River

• Guilford Courthouse

North Carolina

• Cowpens

South Carolina

• Charleston

Georgia   • Savannah

Atlantic Ocean

N
W   E
S

EAST FLORIDA
(SPAIN)

KEY
• Battle site
• Town or fort

In 1777, Howe defeated Washington at Brandywine and Germantown. But Howe was forced to resign for failing to destroy Washington's army and not supporting British general John Burgoyne, who was captured at Saratoga. The new British commander, Sir Henry Clinton, left Philadelphia in mid-1778 and returned to New York. He shifted the action to the South in the hope of pacifying that region.

The greatest battles

In August 1777, Sir William Howe and 15,000 British troops defeated Washington's army of 10,500 at the Brandywine Creek, yet the rebel army remained intact. In October, Washington attacked British encampments at Germantown, Pennsylvania, but his inexperienced army lost to the British. There was still hope, however, as Burgoyne was captured at Saratoga in October. In the winter of 1777–1778, Washington's men trained at Valley Forge. In June, British general Sir Henry Clinton abandoned Philadelphia, sending his army toward New York. Washington attacked him at Monmouth, and the battle ended in a draw. Washington next moved his army to the Hudson Valley to continue the siege of New York City.

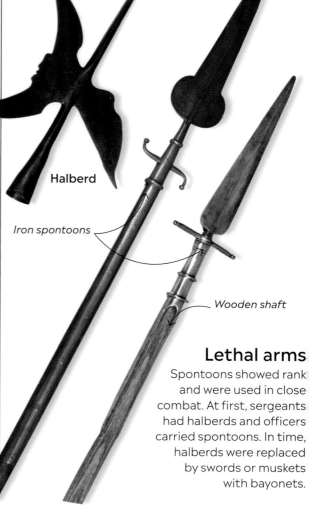

Halberd

Iron spontoons

Wooden shaft

Lethal arms

Spontoons showed rank and were used in close combat. At first, sergeants had halberds and officers carried spontoons. In time, halberds were replaced by swords or muskets with bayonets.

Attack on the Chew House

American assaults at Germantown drove back the enemy, but 120 Redcoats made a stand in the Chews' family house. Heavy fog caused some Americans to fire on each other, resulting in panic, and Washington's army retreated.

Anthony Wayne

Pennsylvanian Wayne was known as "Mad Anthony" because of his reckless spirit. Fighting in several campaigns, he won fame in 1779 for storming Stony Point on the Hudson.

Touch hole pick and brush

Touch hole

Pick *Brush*

Smoothbore musket

Red musket

This smoothbore musket fired a .75-caliber lead ball, accurate to about 75 yards (69 m). The soldier carried a pick and brush to clean residue that clogged the touch hole, which had to be clear for the spark to ignite the charge.

Daniel Morgan

A skilled commander and rifleman, General Morgan served against Burgoyne and Howe in the battles of 1777–1778. His great victory was against a 1,100-strong force in 1781 at Cowpens, South Carolina.

The Battle of Monmouth

Clinton's army of 10,000 men left Philadelphia in June 1778. Washington sent General Charles Lee to attack with 6,400 men, but Lee retreated against Clinton's brigades. Washington and 7,000 men arrived to stop the retreat. Each side lost about 360 men. The Redcoats held the battlefield but withdrew in the night, heading for New York City. Monmouth was the last major battle in the North.

👁 EYEWITNESS

Molly Pitcher
Mary Ludwig Hays (1754–1832) was called "Molly Pitcher" at Monmouth, as she carried water to the soldiers. After her husband was wounded, she took his place. A cannon flew between her knees and tore her skirt. She supposedly said, "Well, that could have been worse," as she continued loading the cannon.

Washington stops Lee's retreat

As General Lee retreated with his division, Washington arrived and demanded to know why. Lee, a former British dragoon officer, claimed his men could not stand against such a formidable enemy. Washington exploded in anger, sent Lee to the back, and hurried his troops into battle order. Lee was court-martialed and suspended from duty.

Victory at
Saratoga

In June 1777, a royal army journeyed from Canada over Lake Champlain. General John Burgoyne led a force of 7,000, including Redcoats and Indigenous warriors. He aimed to capture Albany, New York, and meet the British army operating around New York City. In July, he captured Fort Ticonderoga. They advanced down the Hudson River, but in August part of the army was defeated near Bennington, Vermont. In October, Burgoyne's force surrendered at Saratoga. The American victory convinced France to sign a military alliance with the US: the Treaty of Alliance.

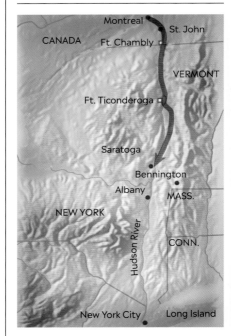

The Lake Champlain-Hudson River region was a strategic military zone. Burgoyne thought he could divide New England from the rest of the colonies by capturing it.

John Burgoyne

The dashing General Burgoyne won the confidence of King George III, who placed him in command of the royal Northern Army for the 1777 campaign. But the Americans surrounded and captured his men at Saratoga, New York.

The fall of General Fraser

The most experienced British officer at Saratoga was General Simon Fraser, who was killed by an American sharpshooter firing from high in a tree. Fraser had served in the colonies through the Seven Years' War and was much loved by his men.

American sharpshooter

General Simon Fraser is shot

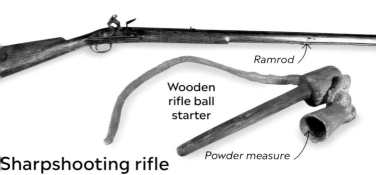

Sharpshooting rifle

Ramrod

Wooden rifle ball starter

Powder measure

The most accurate firearm of the day, rifles were used by rangers and sharpshooters in both armies. A rifle was loaded with black powder poured into the barrel, followed by a lead ball pushed in with a starter and forced all the way down with a ramrod.

EYEWITNESS

Controversial Gates

General Horatio Gates (1727–1806) took credit for the Saratoga victory without acknowledging the role of other commanders, such as Benedict Arnold. It was alleged that he wanted to replace Washington as commander in chief, alluding to him as "one poor Dictator." Blamed for the defeat at the Battle of Camden, he wrote, "I see there has been a premeditated Design to shuffle me out of Service …"

The infamous Arnold

Before Benedict Arnold betrayed the cause of the Revolution and joined the British, he was an excellent American general. While leading a successful attack against German defenders, he was shot and severely wounded in the leg.

A prize of war

Captured British guns were often sent to the artillery-weak American army. This cannon was inscribed with the proud words: "Surrendered by the Convention of Saratoga, October 17, 1777."

Redcoat kettle drum

Each British regiment had musicians that led the way in marches and parades; in battle, they set aside instruments to carry wounded men. This kettle drum of the Ninth Regiment of Foot was captured by the Americans at Saratoga.

Burgoyne offers his sword in defeat

In the painting *Surrender of General Burgoyne* by John Trumbull, Burgoyne is shown offering his sword to General Gates upon surrendering. At right, American officers look on, with royal officers at left. Following military tradition, Gates only touched the sword, then allowed Burgoyne to keep it out of respect for a gallant opponent.

Frontier attacks

Indigenous Americans joined the British to stop American colonists because they feared the colonists would encroach on their lands if they won. Early in the war, loyal Indigenous populations in the South were defeated by Patriots, but in New York's Mohawk Valley, Iroquois under Chief Joseph Brant joined local Loyalists and Redcoats to raid Patriot strongholds. But Virginia frontiersmen, led by George Rogers Clark, invaded the northwest in 1778–1779, capturing the British governor and reducing attacks from that region.

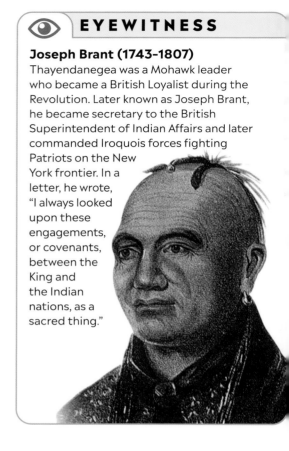
Colonel Louis
Some Indigenous Americans sided with the Continental Army. Akiatonharónkwen, also known as Joseph Louis Cook (seen here with the tomahawk), was a Mohawk. He was the highest-ranking Indigenous fighter in the Continental Army. By supporting the colonists, he fought opposite Joseph Brant.

Tragedy at Oriskany
In 1777, Patriot general Nicholas Herkimer and 800 militiamen tried to protect Fort Stanwix, which had come under attack from the British. En route, Loyalists and allied Indigenous tribes ambushed Herkimer's force near Oriskany, New York, culminating in a bloody battle.

The daring Long Knives

Patriot frontiersmen of Kentucky and western Virginia were nicknamed "Long Knives" because they carried large knives. In 1778, 200 Long Knives led by George Rogers Clark journeyed to the Old Northwest—Ohio, Illinois, and Indiana. Clark captured forts at Vincennes and Kaskaskia and imprisoned Redcoat commander Lieutenant Colonel Henry Hamilton. As a result, the British army held only Fort Detroit in the Northwest.

Round-brimmed hat with feather

The American rifleman
The frontier rifleman was physically tough. He wore a fringed hunting shirt and leggins and carried a tomahawk and long-bladed knife. Respected as sharpshooters and scouts, riflemen roved the forest paths to protect settlements and watch for enemy war parties.

George Rogers Clark
Nicknamed "Conqueror of the Old Northwest," this Virginia frontiersman was a surveyor in the Ohio Valley and Kentucky during the war. He led the region's Patriot militia to defend Northwest settlements against Loyalists and their Indigenous allies.

Hunting knife

Hunting knife
Frontiersmen depended on a good knife for skinning game, preparing food, and for close combat.

Iron blade

Terms of surrender
By marching 20 flags and beating on drums, Clark tricked Hamilton into believing that a Patriot force surrounded the fort. Hamilton soon signed Clark's articles of surrender.

Leggings protect legs and feet

Fort Sackville falls to Clark
In his 1778–1779 campaign, Colonel George Rogers led a winter march to capture Fort Sackville at Vincennes, on the Wabash River. British commander Henry Hamilton surrendered the post to Clark, assuring Patriot control of a vast region that included the future Indiana and Illinois.

Winter soldier

Although both armies usually stayed in quarters during the worst winter weather, Washington was always on the alert for a surprise enemy attack. In the winter of 1778–1779, his little army was weak and hungry when it went into camp at Valley Forge, Pennsylvania. By spring, however, it emerged as a solid fighting force. Since the army usually had a different camp each year, the men also had to build log huts and shelters for livestock, equipment, and supplies.

Baron Friedrich Von Steuben
A Prussian nobleman, Von Steuben joined Washington's army at Valley Forge and drilled troops. He set up a training program for soldiers with and without weapons and even organized their camps.

Von Steuben's manual
Baron Von Steuben wrote a drill manual called *Regulations for the Order and Discipline of the Troops of the United States* that was used to train the entire American army. It was used as the army's drill manual for decades.

Freezing duty
As winter encampments had to be guarded at all times, sentries like this soldier bundled themselves in blanket coats and wrapped their heads and feet in cloth rags.

Ice creepers
Leather strap

Bound with leather straps to shoes or boots, these iron cleats allowed a soldier to cross a frozen surface without slipping.

Visiting the troops
General Washington, left, rides out from headquarters to see how well his men are keeping warm and dry. Accompanied by French volunteer Marquis de Lafayette, Washington makes sure the sentries are alert and on guard, like the soldier standing at attention before him.

Washington's life guard

On duty at a winter encampment, this soldier is a member of the corps that protected General Washington. Called the "Life Guard," this unit of specially chosen men numbered between 180 and 250 during the war.

Officer's trunk

The limited possessions an American officer brought with him could be carried in this leather-covered trunk. The exterior brass tacks protected it during rough handling.

Officer's uniform

The soldier's winter home

A log hut held 12 men, who slept on bunks three high. Loose straw covered with a blanket served as bedding. A soldier's few personal effects included clothing and a Bible.

Mouth harp

This instrument made a twanging sound when it was held between the teeth and the steel vibrator was plucked.

Iron mouth harp

Missing steel vibrator would be here

Building log huts in the snow

It was usually already cold and snow had fallen by the time the army withdrew from the field after a warm-weather campaign. Using oxen, troops had to haul heavy loads and flatten roadways to build huts for their winter encampments.

Symbols of freedom

The early flag of the United States had 13 stripes to represent the colonies, which later became states, and the Union Jack to honor the colonies' British heritage. When independence became the goal, Congress adopted a new flag with a field of stars for the states. Philadelphia's "Liberty Bell," which rang out to celebrate the Declaration of Independence, became a symbol of the Revolution. Another celebration of liberty was "Yankee Doodle," a tune sung by Redcoats that mocked Americans. Patriots composed new verses to express the pride of the revolutionaries.

The first flag
The first American flag was the "Grand Union" flag, combining the British Union Jack and 13 stripes representing the Thirteen Colonies.

Olive branch

National bird
In 1782, the Second Continental Congress adopted the bald eagle as the national bird to appear on the great seal of the US. The bald eagle first appeared on the Massachusetts copper coin in 1776. After much debate, it became a national symbol in 1782.

President John F. Kennedy wrote, "The fierce beauty and proud independence of this great bird aptly symbolizes the strength and freedom of America."

Arrows

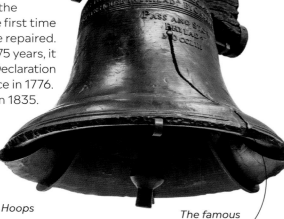

Liberty bell

In 1751, Pennsylvania ordered a bell from England for the new state house. Inscribed "Proclaim Liberty thro' all the land," the bell cracked the first time it was rung and had to be repaired. In use for more than 75 years, it rang joyously for the Declaration of Independence in 1776. It cracked again in 1835.

The famous crack

Song of defiance

Early in the Revolution, Redcoats sang "Yankee Doodle" to mock New England "Yankee" militiamen, calling them "doodles," or fools. When the Yankees triumphed in battle, they insulted the British by singing the "Yankee Doodle" melody with new, patriotic words.

Ropes for tension

Hoops

Leather lugs for tightening ropes

Drum body, painted

Fife and drum of freedom

This military fife was played by militiaman Jonathan Curtis of Concord, Massachusetts. The drum belonged to militiaman William Diamond of Lexington, Massachusetts, who beat out the signal for his companions on Lexington Common on April 19, 1775, where the war's first shots were fired.

Militia fife

Thirteen stars arranged in five rows

Liberty Cap design

Liberty Cap in iron

The knitted "Liberty Cap" was one of the symbols of the American Revolution. Worn as a statement of a radical political position, it was so popular that iron weather vanes were forged into the cap's shape, painted, and fixed proudly to barns and houses.

Walking stick made from crab tree wood

The national colors

In 1777, the new United States needed a "national color" to replace the "Grand Union" flag that bore the Union Jack. On June 14, 1777, Congress resolved that the flag would be 13 stars on a blue field and 13 red and white stripes. They did not agree on a final arrangement of the stars, so various designs were used at first. One had stars in a circle, while others had the stars arranged as seen above.

Painted finish

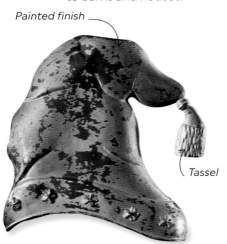

Tassel

Franklin's gift to Washington

Benjamin Franklin specified in his will that his "fine crab tree walking stick with a gold head curiously wrought in the form of a cap of liberty" would be left to his friend General Washington. Franklin died in 1790.

A noble volunteer

In 1777, the modest French nobleman Marquis de Lafayette volunteered to help Washington. He offered to do whatever was needed. An excellent officer, he quickly became a general. Washington was fond of Lafayette and treated him like a son.

French alliance

Short on military supplies, cash, and a navy, America needed allies. After losing the Seven Years' War, France was eager to help America. By mid-1776, France was secretly sending financial aid and supplies to support the Revolution, but more was needed. That year, Benjamin Franklin traveled to Paris along with Arthur Lee and Silas Deane to arrange a formal alliance with King Louis XVI. The Americans befriended the foreign minister Comte de (Count of) Vergennes, who masterminded France's efforts. France was the first country to recognize the US, after both countries signed the Treaty of Alliance. By early 1778, a state of war existed between France and Britain. Eventually, more than 12,000 French troops would fight in America under commander Comte de Rochambeau.

Golden Louis

This French louis d'or gold piece and thousands more just like it arrived in America as a gift from France. The valuable "Louis" helped turn the tide in favor of the Revolution.

Crown

Image of King Louis XVI

Fleur-de-lis

French royal symbol

The fleur-de-lis, or "lily flower," decorated the coat of arms of the French royal house of the Bourbons.

Franklin at the French court

Scientist, philosopher, and diplomat, Benjamin Franklin was famous throughout France and warmly welcomed when he and the American delegation arrived in 1777. They were presented at the royal palace of Versailles to King Louis XVI, who approved aid to help the Revolution.

John Adams inspects French marines

The French army included several regiments of Irish-born troops, who often wore red uniforms. In this painting, American diplomat John Adams is inspecting Irishmen on the coast of France. They have volunteered as marines for the American warship *Bonhomme Richard*.

French sword

There were many types and sizes of swords, from the cavalryman's heavy saber to this light and slender French "small sword," ideal for an infantry officer.

White metal blade

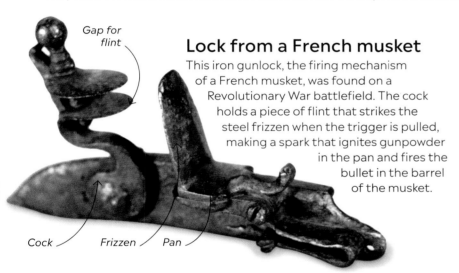

Gap for flint

Lock from a French musket

This iron gunlock, the firing mechanism of a French musket, was found on a Revolutionary War battlefield. The cock holds a piece of flint that strikes the steel frizzen when the trigger is pulled, making a spark that ignites gunpowder in the pan and fires the bullet in the barrel of the musket.

Cock   Frizzen   Pan

The French commander

The leader of French troops in North America, Jean Baptiste Donatien de Vimeur, Comte de Rochambeau, commanded more than 7,000 well-equipped French soldiers. He treated Washington and the Americans as equals: at one point, Rochambeau opened his army's war chest to Washington, offering to share half of the money it held.

Comte de Vergennes

French foreign minister Charles Gravier, Comte de Vergennes, helped with secret contributions of funds and supplies to the American revolutionaries. France's support of America led to all-out war in 1778.

The war at sea

Americans lacked warships but soon tried a new invention: the submarine. In 1776, the *Turtle* attempted to attach a bomb beneath a warship in New York Harbor, but when the plan failed, submarines were forgotten for decades. British ships dominated American waters until the French fleet arrived to challenge them in 1778. While huge sea battles raged between French and British fleets in Caribbean and European waters, the Americans had triumphs of their own. Congress authorized private ship owners, called "privateers," to attack enemy vessels.

UNDERWATER ATTACK

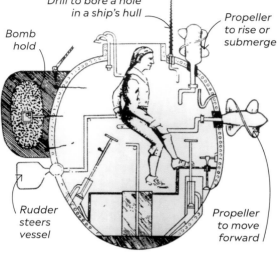

Drill to bore a hole in a ship's hull

Propeller to rise or submerge

Bomb hold

Rudder steers vessel

Propeller to move forward

The first combat submarine, called the *Turtle*, was invented by engineer David Bushnell. It went into action in September 1776 in New York Harbor. Its one-man crew tried unsuccessfully to attach a bomb to the hull of a British warship.

A French admiral

In 1778, Admiral Charles Comte d'Estaing failed to seal off New York Harbor. Next, he refused to aid an American attack on Rhode Island, and he could not wipe out weaker enemy squadrons in the Caribbean. He was wounded in a defeat at Savannah in 1779.

Recruiting poster for Paul Jones' ship *Ranger* in 1777

Naval flags

The British Royal Navy's red flag has a Union Jack in the corner. Independent states designed flags for their own warships. For example, South Carolina's ships carried flags with a rattlesnake and a stern warning.

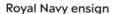

Royal Navy ensign

Similar to Benjamin Franklin's "Join, or Die" illustration, which also features a snake

South Carolina naval flag

DONT TREAD ON ME

Enlist now!

Posters called for sailors to enlist with commander John Paul Jones. Officers and crew shared the money made from captured and sold enemy vessels.

The *Raleigh*

The 32-gun frigate *Raleigh* was one of the 13-ship fleet of the first Continental Navy. Frigates were fast, medium-sized warships carrying between 28 and 60 guns. *Raleigh* was captured by the British, who copied its design for their own vessels.

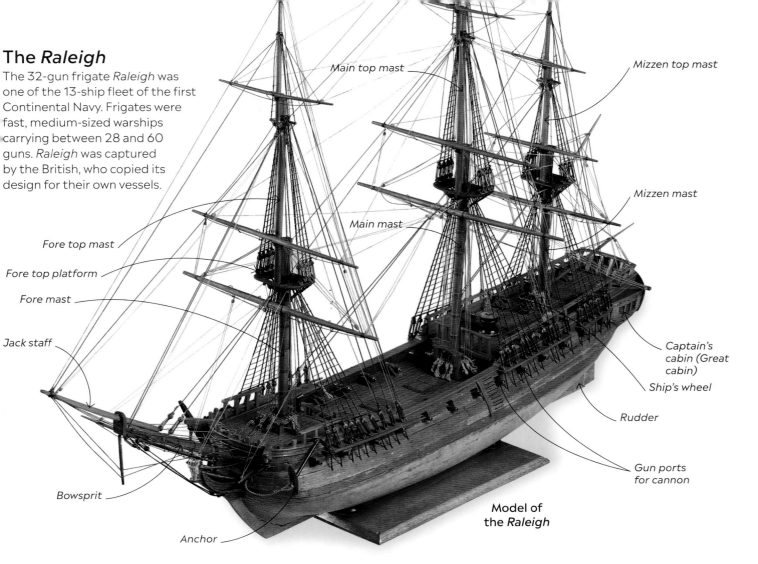

Main top mast

Mizzen top mast

Fore top mast

Main mast

Mizzen mast

Fore top platform

Fore mast

Jack staff

Captain's cabin (Great cabin)

Ship's wheel

Rudder

Gun ports for cannon

Bowsprit

Model of the *Raleigh*

Anchor

A battle to the death

In 1779, John Paul Jones led his *Bonhomme Richard* in the Battle of Flamborough Head with the enemy's flagship, *Serapis*—misspelled "*Seraphis*" in the artwork (right). As the British captain saw the American ship sinking, he demanded that Jones surrender. Jones answered, "I have not yet begun to fight!" He captured the *Serapis* as his own vessel went down. In 1787, Congress honored Jones with a medal for his service.

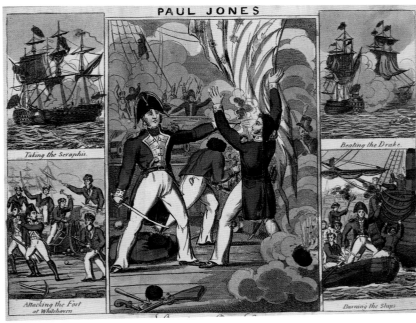

Scenes from the career of John Paul Jones
The central image shows Jones—America's first well-known naval officer—attacking one of his officers, who wanted to surrender during battle with the *Serapis*. Jones seized the enemy ship (top left).

Revolutionary warship

John Paul Jones

1787 John Paul Jones Congressional gold medal

Embattled New York

Symbols of resistance
Before the Revolution, Patriots and Redcoats clashed in New York City. Liberty Poles (wooden poles topped by a Liberty Cap) were raised by the Sons of Liberty and torn down by soldiers after bloody fights. The poles were symbols of dissent against British rule.

In 1775, Patriot activists were outnumbered by Loyalists in New York City. After losing Boston early in 1776, Sir William Howe captured New York that summer, driving out Washington and the rebel sympathizers. Patriots burned down part of New York, but Redcoats held on to the city for the rest of the war. Thousands of Loyalists came, causing overcrowding and food shortages. After peace was made, on November 25, 1783, Washington and his few remaining officers rode in to take back New York—the last port to be evacuated by the British.

Downing the king's statue
In July 1776, the Declaration of Independence was read to the American army in New York and a mob tore down a statue of King George.

Sir Henry Clinton
Known for his bravery, Clinton was Howe's top lieutenant general during the invasion of New York in 1776. In 1778, he succeeded Howe in overall command, but he resigned in 1781 after failing to achieve victory over the revolutionaries.

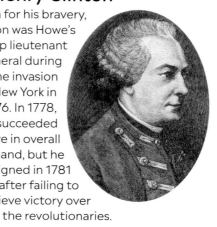

German troops help the British
In 1776, German soldiers captured New York, then occupied Manhattan.

The Great Fire

As the British moved into New York in 1776, Washington wanted to prevent use of the city as a British base. Although it is not known if direct orders were given, rebels soon set fire to much of New York.

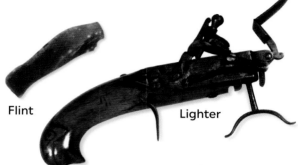

Flint

Lighter

Tinder lighter

This lighter sparked to ignite tinder, a flammable material kept dry in a box. Burning tinder ignited kindling to start a fire. A steel striker was struck against flint to create a spark.

Tinder box

Steel striker

Fire and terror
As buildings in New York burned on September 21, 1776, British soldiers beat and bayoneted suspected arsonists. For years to come, there were not enough houses for occupying soldiers and civilians.

Flying the Stars and Stripes

British soldiers leaving New York nailed the Union Jack to a flagpole. While Redcoats watched, a Patriot climbed up, tore off the flag, and put up the Stars and Stripes instead.

Triumphant entry into the city

On November 25, 1783, or "Evacuation Day," Washington and some officers took possession of New York City from the departing British.

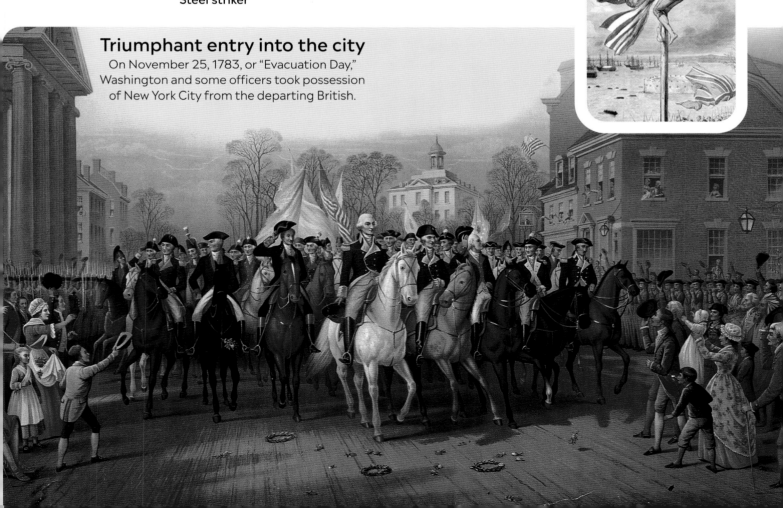

Spies and traitors

During the Revolution, secret messages were sometimes written in code and often hidden in shoe heels. Captured spies were hanged, such as the 20-year-old Continental officer Nathan Hale, who was caught in New York in 1776. Through much of the war, Washington counted on Major Benjamin Tallmadge to meet secretly with undercover agents and give them money. New Jersey-born Patience Wright, who lived in England during the war, hid messages inside her own sculptures and shipped them to American Patriots. General Benedict Arnold was the most notorious traitor to the Revolution. His plan to surrender West Point in 1780 was uncovered just in time.

A Patriot's cloak

During Washington's 1775–1776 siege of Boston, Deborah Champion wore this hooded cloak to carry messages and the army payroll secretly to rebel troops there.

Ring of spies

Benjamin Tallmadge was the leader of the Culper Ring, Washington's group of spies. It included Robert Townsend, Anna Strong, and others. Tallmadge provided Washington intelligence from British headquarters in New York City and exposed Benedict Arnold's plot.

Coins for conspiracies

There were very few coins in Revolutionary America, and what there were included Spanish silver reales, sometimes cut into several pieces. Spies had to be paid, and secret messengers needed cash to buy horses or pay for ferries or food, so any silver money would do.

His life for liberty

In mid-1776, Patriot spy Nathan Hale slipped into occupied New York City disguised as a schoolmaster. Caught and then sentenced to be hanged, legend has it he said, "I regret that I have but one life to give for my country!"

Hollow bullet

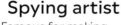

A piece of paper with a message from one British commander to another was folded and concealed in this hollow silver bullet.

Spying artist

Famous for making heads out of putty or wax, American Patience Wright owned a studio in London. As a supporter of the rebel cause, she talked to her subjects about British military plans, then passed on to Patriot agents whatever she learned.

A traitor revealed
On September 21, 1780, General Benedict Arnold secretly handed documents outlining fortifications and troop information to British major John André. With the message hidden in the heel of his boot, André was on his way back to British lines when he was stopped by rebel sentries. He was hanged as a spy.

The capture of Major John André, seen here with papers that have been recovered from his boot

Fallen hero

With such success on the battlefield, General Arnold despised Congress for placing other officers ahead of him in rank. In 1780, the disillusioned general conspired to help the British capture West Point. When the plot was discovered, he escaped to join the British forces. He eventually went to England with his wife and children.

Document box
Important papers, military dispatches, and correspondence needed to be sheltered from the elements and prying eyes. This leather, brass, and canvas strongbox could be locked securely to protect its contents.

Plotting together
Benedict Arnold's wife, Philadelphian Peggy (Shippen) Arnold, was a Loyalist and the highest-paid spy during the Revolution. Actively involved in her husband's espionage plot, she was the link between him and the head of the British Secret Service.

Benedict Arnold
Once immensely popular, in 1780 Arnold became the most hated turncoat when he tried to arrange the British capture of West Point in exchange for £20,000. He escaped and joined the royal forces, then left America for Britain in 1781.

The home front

During the Revolution, Americans were divided into three camps: Patriots, Loyalists, and neutrals. Only a few thousand people on each side made up the armies. Loyalists, who were around 20 percent of the American population, gathered in cities that were British strongholds, while Patriots gained control of most of the countryside. Neutrals were often harassed by both armies, and in land between the hostile forces no one was safe from raiders and pillagers. Yet life went on and families worked hard to survive and make the best of things. Some even continued to meet their neighbors at their local public house.

Hoeing the land
To keep weeds down, farmers worked the soil with iron hoes attached to stout handles.

Farm work goes on
Most Americans lived on farms during the Revolution, and planting and harvesting continued according to the seasons. The crops depended on the simple plow, held by the farmer while draft animals pulled.

Redcoat pillaging
Although soldiers were not encouraged to raid farmsteads and steal from houses, they often did. These Redcoats, below, are ransacking a house in New Jersey while the distraught family looks on.

Meeting places

Taverns and inns (or "public houses") and coffeehouses were places where folk gathered to drink and eat, read newspapers, share stories, gossip, and gamble on dice and cards. They also offered room and board for travelers. Political meetings were often held in such places.

A favorite pipe
At public houses, the end pieces of clay pipes were broken off so the next guest would have a fresh stem to smoke.

Corkscrew

Wooden staves

Hungry for news
Patrons of a New York City coffeehouse read the newspapers, which might consist of recent editions published in the British-occupied city, month-old papers from England, or journals from rebel-held New Jersey.

Green-lead glass bottle

Fill hole

Iron hoops bind wooden staves

Hearth and home

Home life centered on the hearth, where food was cooked and hands were warmed. The hearth might be made of brick, cut stone, or dried clay, but it always had to have a ready supply of kindling and firewood. Women found it hard to sustain their families with the men away at war. Many chose to follow their husbands to the battlefields, working as nurses, cooks, and cleaners.

Fitted bodice

Brown tabby silk material

The family meal
The women of the house were in charge of the kitchen and the hearth and spent many hours preparing food, preserving fruits and vegetables, drying herbs, and smoking meat.

Simple, practical fashion
The woman's everyday dress of the period had a close-fitting bodice above a petticoat and full overskirt. This allowed freedom of movement while modestly concealing the woman's ankles.

Camps and prisons

Candle lantern
Iron lanterns were carried around or suspended on a hook. They gave off little light, but few people went out after dark anyway.

Door for replacing or extinguishing candle

Always short of money, both Congress and Parliament tried to avoid war expenses. This meant ignoring the needs of prisoners, who were often treated inhumanely. British prison ships were notoriously cruel, as were Patriot prison camps. Unfortunately, enlisted soldiers were also often badly treated. While British soldiers were far better fed and equipped than Americans, both depended on their camp followers to give them comfort. The women and merchants following the armies provided food, drink, and welcome companionship to the off-duty soldier.

Locked in a tower
A former Congress president, Henry Laurens was captured in 1780. He was thrown into the Tower of London and threatened with execution. Exchanged for General Cornwallis, Laurens went to Paris as a peace delegate.

Coin shows a sundial, below which is written "Mind your business"

Worthless money
The Continental Congress issued a new form of currency—paper money—to fund the war. But many did not want "Continental" money because if the rebels lost the war, it would become worthless. It lost its value due to reasons such as fake notes being circulated.

Unloading supplies
Military encampments required a steady flow of loaded wagons to feed, clothe, shelter, and equip the troops. Sturdy Conestoga wagons pulled by teams of four to six oxen or horses were capable of hauling 15,000 lb (6,800 kg) of cargo over rough roads.

The fortunes of war

Prisons for the enlisted men of both sides were unhealthy, brutal places. The average soldier was often left to rot for years, with a slim chance for survival or recovery. Officers were, however, treated far better and were usually exchanged for an enemy prisoner of equal rank.

Caverns called "Hell"
In Newgate, Connecticut, Loyalist prisoners were forced to work deep underground in copper mines and caverns they nicknamed "Hell." Hundreds of prisoners became extremely ill, and many died.

The cruel prison ships
Patriot prisoners in the New York area were crammed into old ships anchored around the city. These "prison hulks," such as the *Jersey*, anchored off Brooklyn, were damp, filthy, and cold, causing hundreds of starved prisoners to become ill and die.

Following the troops

Many civilians stayed close to the armies. These "camp followers" included wives and children of soldiers and merchants who sold wares to the troops. When not marching or fighting, soldiers had considerable freedom to visit their families among the camp followers, enjoying meals that were better than army fare.

Spoon carved from deer antler

Brass fork with wooden handle

Eating utensils
With long hours in camp, soldiers had time to carve bone and horn and whittle wood. They made utensils and cups, which were needed to replace utensils lost while campaigning.

Gridiron for cooking over campfire

Carved initials, "WCW"

Drinking cup made from a horn

Legs to stand over flame

Cooking for the troops
Camp followers were also found near prisoner-of-war enclosures, and a certain amount of communication was allowed between captives and their families. These folk cooked on open fires in their own encampments, often selling food to captive and sentry alike.

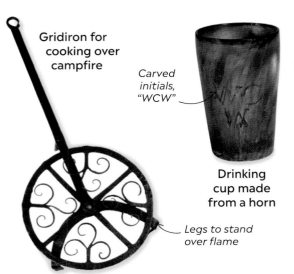

The soldier's doctor

In 1775, the colonies had about 3,500 doctors. The leading Patriot physician, Dr. Benjamin Rush of Philadelphia, wrote a manual on keeping soldiers healthy, but diseases like smallpox, typhus, and malaria killed 10 times more people than injuries sustained in battle. Hospitals were short-staffed and lacked supplies, medicine, and nutritious food. Conditions were primitive: surgical tools for extracting bullets, amputating limbs, and drawing blood were not sterilized. Many men died from minor wounds that became infected. In time, better hospitals were designed, improving chances for recovery.

Leather carrying case

Lancet and case
This two-bladed lancet has pointed double-edged blades used for bloodletting and cutting veins. The lancet was also used for opening up infections to drain them.

Battlefield aid
A soldier groans while his wound is bandaged, as anesthesia was unknown in Revolutionary times. Officers received rum, brandy, or opium to dull the pain. Also, the small chest of medical supplies would not have contained antiseptic for cleaning wounds, since this was not yet known to doctors.

Steel lancet blades

The apothecary's art

Apothecaries made, mixed, and sold drugs, but most families used homegrown medicinal herbs. For serious illnesses, such as malaria, the apothecary used imported drugs.

Improved hospitals

Replacing crowded sick chambers in tents and private homes, this Valley Forge hospital allowed the free flow of air, which helped improve patients' health.

Portable medicine chest

Military physicians kept wooden chests containing medicines, syringes, sponges, forceps, bandages, twine, and pharmaceutical equipment for weighing and mixing ingredients. Doctors had access only to common medicines like mercury compounds, lavender spirits, cream of tartar, and opium. Hospitals used large chests, with 80 or more different medicines, while regimental surgeons in the field carried smaller chests.

Side compartments swing open on hinges, showing more storage space

Compartments for storing medicines

Medicine bottle

Cupping glass

Medical equipment

Old bandages were pulled apart by iron forceps to see if the wound was healing. Placing a glass cup against the skin—"cupping"—drew blood and pus to the surface. A pewter bowl caught blood and fluids.

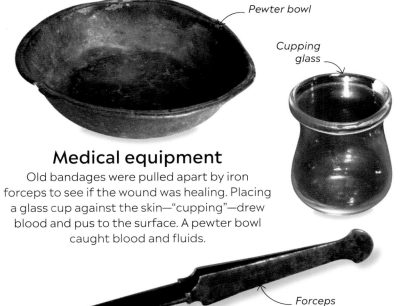

Pewter bowl

Cupping glass

Forceps

The British won most battles in the South, including Savannah, Charleston, and Camden. Still, Commander Greene organized fresh resistance wherever the enemy marched.

War for the South

Late in 1778, the war shifted to the South, as the British captured Savannah, Georgia. In the spring of 1780, Charleston, South Carolina, also fell to royal forces. General Cornwallis and his army soon destroyed an American force at Camden, South Carolina, resulting in the removal of Horatio Gates as commander in the Southern Department of the war. George Washington sent Nathanael Greene of Rhode Island to take charge in the South. In March 1781, Cornwallis defeated Greene at Guilford Courthouse, North Carolina, but suffered great losses. Cornwallis withdrew to the sea, and eventually to Yorktown, Virginia, to await support that never came.

Hilt

Iron blade, 35 in (89 cm) long

Horseman's saber

This heavy, curved sword, called a saber, belonged to an American cavalryman. A trooper learned to use the saber while also managing a horse—practicing slashes and thrusts and blocking opponents' blades.

Bright red fabric cut from the back of a chair

Dragoon flag

This flag was carried into the Battle of Cowpens by Colonel William Washington's dragoons, who followed it to a spectacular victory.

The Roman numeral "VII" shows this is the flag of the 7th Fusiliers

EYEWITNESS

Spanish hero

Bernardo de Gálvez (1746-1786), governor of Spanish Louisiana, defeated the British at Pensacola in 1781. He freed the lower Mississippi Valley region from the British. He was awarded honorary US citizenship as a "hero ... who risked his life for the freedom of the United States people and provided supplies, intelligence, and strong military support ..."

Captured colors

At Cowpens, General Daniel Morgan's troops captured the regimental flag of the British 7th Fusiliers. More than 320 British soldiers either died or were wounded, while 600 others were imprisoned. In contrast, 22 Americans were killed and 60 wounded.

Regimental badge

Cavalry fight at Cowpens, South Carolina

British dragoons surrounded American commander Colonel William Washington, center. His servant, left, fired a pistol and saved his life. Tarleton's 1,100-man British and Loyalist army was wiped out by an American force of about the same size under General Daniel Morgan. This and the Loyalist militia's defeat at the Battle of Kings Mountain convinced Cornwallis to leave South Carolina.

Servant rescuing William Washington

The key to final victory

One of Washington's best generals in the South, Nathanael Greene kept his men fighting and avoided crushing defeats. While the British army pursued him, other rebel commanders attacked enemy supply lines and forts. By late 1781, almost all British posts outside Charleston and Savannah had been abandoned.

Winning the South
Nathanael Greene commanded rebel forces in the South. He inflicted very heavy losses on Cornwallis, who withdrew to Yorktown in 1781, hoping for reinforcements.

Victory in defeat
In 1781, Greene's force of 4,400 Continentals and militia took on Cornwallis's 1,900 men at Guilford Courthouse, North Carolina. After the furious battle, Cornwallis held the field but suffered more than 500 casualties. Greene lost fewer men—78 were killed and 183 wounded.

Shot bags
Revolutionary militia soldiers sometimes took hunting firearms into battle. These leather shot bags held five bird-shot balls.

Plug top

Cartridge box
This brass cartridge box was probably once the property of a German soldier. It kept ammunition safe and dry.

Lid

Forest motifs

Yorktown

By August 1781, Cornwallis and his 7,500 veterans were at Yorktown, Virginia, waiting for reinforcements and supplies from British-held New York. Washington and French general de Rochambeau moved to trap Cornwallis, and the French fleet arrived to blockade Yorktown. The Franco-American armies numbered more than 17,000 troops. The British fleet arrived in September, but the French admiral de Grasse drove it back to New York. Washington fired devastating artillery barrages day after day, until Cornwallis gave up. On October 19, the defeated royal army marched out of Yorktown. This was the last major battle of the Revolution.

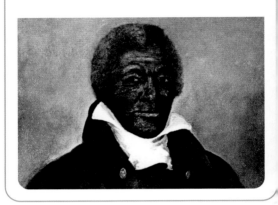

Pocket telescope
Telescopes were essential for military leaders to view enemy troop movements. They were also used on ships to observe flag signals from friendly vessels.

Eyepiece

Lens

Screw cap protects lens

Sir Samuel Hood
British Admiral Hood, alongside Admiral Thomas Graves, could not prevent the French navy from blockading Cornwallis, who was trapped.

Francois de Grasse
French warships under Admiral de Grasse landed 3,000 soldiers to help besiege the British at Yorktown in September 1781. When enemy ships appeared, de Grasse fought them off.

The decisive sea battle
Admiral de Grasse beat British admirals Hood and Graves at the Battle of the Chesapeake Capes on September 15, forcing them back to New York. If the British navy had brought reinforcements or rescued Cornwallis, this campaign could have turned in favor of the British.

Storming the Yorktown redoubt

Washington moved his trenches and artillery closer to the British fortifications by digging new works under cover of darkness. On October 14, Captain Alexander Hamilton led a nighttime assault against a British redoubt, while French infantry attacked another. Eventually, Cornwallis had to surrender.

The deadly bayonet

At the start of the Revolution, a bayonet wielded by a Redcoat was the most feared of weapons. By the war's end, elite American troops were also skilled in bayonet attacks. This was how they captured a key stronghold at Yorktown.

During the surrender, the British band played
"The World Turned Upside Down."

Match rope

Spear point

Iron linstock piece is 14 in (36 cm) long

Wooden shaft

Charles Cornwallis

Lord Cornwallis won battles but could not destroy the rebels. After the war, he became governor general of India and a high official in the British government.

Artilleryman's linstock

Gunners at Yorktown used a linstock like this to hold the match that fired a cannon. The match was brought to the touch hole, igniting the gunpowder that fired the charge.

Washington's greatest victory

Claiming illness, Cornwallis did not attend the surrender ceremonies. His second-in-command, Charles O'Hara, offered his sword to Washington. He refused it and directed Benjamin Lincoln to accept the sword.

57

The last two years of war

Although the battles ended with Yorktown, the war would not be over until the peace treaty was signed. There were small clashes, and men still died. Washington promised to remain in the field until New York City, the last Redcoat foothold, was evacuated. Through much of 1782–1783, he was with his army near Newburgh, New York. Still, his officers and men were angry that Congress was unable to provide the back pay it owed them. So, in part to lift their spirits, Washington created a decoration, later known as the "Purple Heart."

Loss of life continues

A much-admired aide to Washington, Colonel John Laurens was killed during a minor clash near Charleston in his native South Carolina. Laurens was the son of Henry Laurens, former president of Congress.

Meigs's hat

Connecticut militiaman Phineas Meigs was 74 when he answered an alarm in 1782. As a British warship was raiding East Guilford, he was shot in the head. He was one of the last to die in the Revolution.

Bullet hole

Various caliber lead bullets

The official seal

Congress agreed in 1782 on a concept for America's seal, based on Secretary of Congress Charles Thomson's sketch (left). The motto "E Pluribus Unum" means "Out of many, one."

Olive branch shows the US strives for peace

Arrows symbolize that the US is ready for war

Hudson headquarters

Washington could have gone home to Mount Vernon during the winter of 1782–1783, but he stayed with the army instead. The Americans were based close to Newburgh, New York, about 50 miles (80 km) north of British-held New York City. The general lived in the Hasbrouck house, next to the Hudson River.

Troops return home

The Continental Army was disbanded in stages during 1783. Although officially discharged, they did not get the back pay owed to them because Congress lacked the funds. The troops were discharged a few at a time to avoid an angry mass mutiny by the unhappy men. Many returned home embittered that Congress had not kept its promises. Years would pass before the soldiers received their long-deserved pay and pensions.

A Loyalist's coat
Munson Hoyt of Norwalk, Connecticut, owner of this coat, was a Loyalist lieutenant. He relocated to New Brunswick, Canada, but eventually returned to live in the United States.

Farewells at New Windsor
Revolutionary troops above leave their quarters at New Windsor, New York. The Hudson Highlands in the background provided them with a strong position to prevent the British from striking northward from New York City.

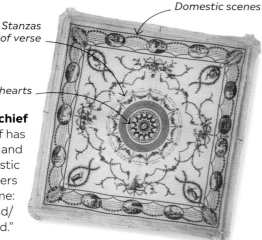

Stanzas of verse
Domestic scenes
Thirteen hearts

Liberty handkerchief
This printed linen handkerchief has 13 hearts for the new states and bears illustrations of domestic scenes. Its 13 verses honor soldiers at war and families working at home: "While they our Liberties defend/ Let us to Husbandry attend."

Sir Guy Carleton
Carleton replaced Clinton as the commander of British forces in America. Carleton worked closely with Washington to arrange a peaceful evacuation of Redcoats from New York in November 1783.

The purple heart

Washington created a "Badge of Military Merit" to award soldiers for outstanding acts of courage. Only three such badges were awarded, all in 1783. This badge was almost forgotten until 1932, the 200th anniversary of Washington's birth, when it was revived as the "Purple Heart," a decoration for people wounded in action.

Badge of Military Merit
Washington awards the new badges at his Newburgh, New York, headquarters in 1783. Sergeant William Brown receives his badge, while Sergeant Elijah Churchill awaits. Sergeant Daniel Bissell was honored later.

Sketch of the original badge

Badge of Military Merit

A new nation
emerges

Peace negotiations between British and American delegates began in mid-1782 in Paris. The final 1783 Treaty of Paris recognized the independence of the United States, with the Mississippi River as its western boundary. It took several years for a Constitution to be drafted. A key leader and political thinker during this period was James Madison, who helped write and pass the Constitution. Hamilton, Madison, and Jay authored a collection of 85 essays known as *The Federalist Papers*, arguing in favor of the Constitution. They were published in newspapers to encourage public support for the document. The Constitution of the United States was drafted in 1787, ratified in 1788, and went into effect on March 4, 1789 as the central law of the new nation.

John Adams became the first president to reside in the White House

Henry Laurens is the only American to have been held in the Tower of London in England

Provisional agreement

In November 1782, a provisional peace treaty to end the Revolutionary War was signed by the negotiators. The final document was approved on September 3, 1783, and named the Treaty of Paris.

American peacemakers

Artist Benjamin West painted portraits of the American peace negotiators in Paris to include them in a larger painting along with British negotiators. However, the British refused to pose, so West left them out of this picture. The Americans are, from left to right, John Jay, John Adams, Benjamin Franklin, Henry Laurens, and William Temple Franklin, their secretary.

General Lincoln's teapot

This teapot includes the symbol of the Society of the Cincinnati, a fraternity of Revolutionary officers. It bears the initials "BL," honoring General Benjamin Lincoln.

Washington submits his resignation

At the height of his glory as a conquering hero, George Washington faithfully returned his commander in chief's commission to members of Congress assembled at Annapolis, Maryland, on December 23, 1783.

The Constitution

On September 17, 1787, representatives of the 13 states met in Philadelphia to approve an official Constitution, which provided for a stronger central government, unlike the Articles of Confederation (1781), which gave the states more powers. The document was declared "the supreme law of the land."

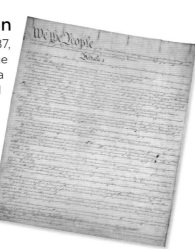

TERRITORIAL CLAIMS

THE UNITED STATES
After the Treaty of 1783
Showing the claims of the older States
to the Western Lands.

Many states claimed to own western lands, but these claims were eventually turned over to the federal government in exchange for the federal government assuming their debts from the Revolutionary War. This map shows those claims in a tint of the same color as that of the claiming state.

👁 EYEWITNESS

Father of the Constitution

James Madison (1751–1836) wrote, "The people are the only legitimate fountain of power, and it is from them that the constitutional charter ... is derived." He drafted the Bill of Rights, containing 10 Constitutional amendments, by adapting George Mason's Virginia Declaration of Rights.

Revolutionary financier

Philadelphia merchant Robert Morris headed the Continental Congress's Department of Finance during the war. He, along with Hamilton, helped lay the foundation for the financial operations of the US. He set up the Bank of North America in 1781.

George Washington

Early in December 1783, Washington bade farewell to his officers. A few weeks later, he resigned his commission before Congress and rode back to his wife, Martha, at Mount Vernon. In 1789, Washington was unanimously elected the first president of the United States, and he served two terms from 1789 to 1797. After his presidency, Washington enjoyed the life of a Virginia planter. On December 14, 1799, he died at Mount Vernon. Precedents set by him—such as serving only two terms after being elected and returning to civilian life after the presidency—are followed to this day.

Washington's .65-caliber flintlock pistols

Silver decoration with the lion and the unicorn

The general's pistols
Washington owned this pair of silver-mounted pistols during the Revolution. Made in England, they bear designs that include the lion and the unicorn.

Washington in victory
Patriot artist Charles Willson Peale created this image of the general a few months after the 1779 liberation of Philadelphia. The painting commemorates Washington's victory at Princeton two years earlier.

Bidding farewell

On December 4, 1783—after the British evacuated New York City—Washington and his officers gathered at Fraunces Tavern. He thanked them for their "glorious and honorable" service. Then he rode to Annapolis, Maryland, and resigned as commander in chief. On this journey, people lined the roads to see him.

The Fraunces Tavern Museum

Washington's farewell to his officers in Fraunces Tavern

Signing the Constitution

Washington was elected presiding officer of the Constitutional Convention in Philadelphia. On September 28, 1787, as pictured on the right, the delegates signed the document. In 1789, Washington became the first president of the United States.

Stately Mount Vernon
Washington's brother, Lawrence, built the estate Mount Vernon. Washington expanded the estate and moved there with his wife, Martha, after they were married.

Home at Mount Vernon

Whether in military headquarters or serving as the United States president, Washington often longed to be with Martha at Mount Vernon. He loved his estate that overlooked the Potomac River, managing Mount Vernon's agriculture, selecting the crops, and planning development. The Washingtons were the guardians of two of their grandchildren, who enriched their home life.

George Washington's grandchildren

Reflector

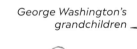

The Virginia planter
Washington enjoyed working on his plantation. Mount Vernon's fields were tended by slaves, who—in accord with Washington's will—were given their freedom after he and Martha died.

Martha Custis Washington
Martha Washington was known for her kindness, wisdom, and patriotism. During the American Revolution, she regularly spent time at army camps with Washington.

Washington's candelabrum

Porcelain serving dish from Mount Vernon

Did you know?

FASCINATING FACTS

In 1778, John Adams took his young son, John Quincy Adams, with him to England. In 1781, at age 14, the younger Adams was appointed secretary and translator to the US commissioner to the Court of Russia.

Young John Quincy Adams

During the Revolution, soldiers tore paper out of books to use as wadding to clean out their rifles.

Rebels imprisoned Benjamin Franklin's son William, Royal Governor of New Jersey. He remained a Loyalist and fled to England in 1782.

In 1775, Benjamin Franklin wrote a Declaration of Independence. It would be another year before Congress would ask Thomas Jefferson to write his version—with Franklin's help.

Although it is not certain that Betsy Ross sewed the first American flag, she did mend uniforms and make tents, blankets, musket balls, and gun cartridges.

On April 26, 1777, Sybil Ludington, age 16, rode 20 miles (32 km) to alert her father's militia company that Danbury, Connecticut, was under attack and to gather at the Ludington house. George Washington later thanked her.

Many women came under fire in war, like Margaret Corbin, who was wounded serving in the Battle of Fort Washington on November 16, 1776.

Most people know about the Boston Tea Party of 1773. But few people remember that on March 7, 1774, protesters dumped more tea in the harbor at a second "party."

In 1776, Americans had the highest standard of living and the lowest taxes in the Western world.

Washington owned at least 577 slaves over the course of his life.

Approximately 6-12 percent of Washington's army was made up of Black men.

Two brothers from Virginia, Richard Henry Lee and Francis Lightfoot Lee, were among the signers of the Declaration of Independence. Their cousin, Revolutionary War commander Henry Lee, was the father of Robert E. Lee, who would command the Confederate Army during the American Civil War.

Indigo blue

American uniform

The American uniforms during the war were blue because indigo was one of the most common dyes available in the colonies.

Before the Battle of Trenton, a boy handed Colonel Johann Gottlieb Rall a note warning that Washington was about to attack. He put the note in his pocket unopened; it was found after he was killed in the battle.

In a letter to her husband John Adams, Abigail Adams wrote, "Remember the ladies ... Do not put such unlimited power into the hands of the husbands. Remember, all men would be tyrants if they could."

The Battle of Rhode Island

QUESTIONS AND ANSWERS

What is the Society of the Cincinnati?

Officers who served in the Continental Army founded this society to promote liberty and national honor. It is named after Cincinnatus, a Roman dictator who famously relinquished power after ending a crisis. Washington was often compared to him because he, too, gave up power and returned to life as a farmer. He was elected president of the society but later resigned after he grew skeptical of the hereditary-based organization.

Bald eagle

Society of the Cincinnati medal

Why did King George III of England nearly abdicate the throne?

Parliament did not adhere to the king's wish to fight after Yorktown. So the king wrote a letter of abdication, but later withdrew it. When he learned that Washington would resign, the king exclaimed, "If he does that, Sir, he will be the greatest man in the world!"

Where did the song "Yankee Doodle" come from?

Richard Shuckburgh, an English surgeon in New York, is thought to have written some of the most famous verses. His "Yankey Song" made fun of New England militiamen in the Seven Years' War. The term "Yankee" comes from the Dutch word "Janke," or "Johnny." "Doodle" meant fool, or clown. By 1776, the Patriots had their own version.

When was the first official name given to the United States?

On September 9, 1776, the Continental Congress officially declared the name of the new nation the United States of North America. Two years later, Congress officially decided to shorten the name to the United States of America.

When did the eagle become an American symbol?

The bald eagle became an official symbol in 1782. Congress put it on the Great Seal of the United States.

Why is there a monument to an unnamed soldier's left leg on the battlefield at Saratoga?

Although he later helped the British, Benedict Arnold was a great American hero at Saratoga. During the battle, a bullet shattered his left leg. A monument was built at Saratoga to honor him, but it was unnamed, since he was by then considered a traitor.

Which one of Washington's children died at the Battle of Yorktown?

Washington did not have children of his own, but he adopted Martha's children after their

John Parke Custis

marriage. His adopted son, John "Jackie" Parke Custis, was an aide to Washington at the Battle of Yorktown. Sadly, he died of camp fever after the battle ended.

Did George Washington really have wooden teeth?

No. According to legend, he never smiled in paintings because he was embarrassed about his wooden teeth. As he had terrible toothaches, his real teeth were replaced with false, but not wooden, ones. During his life, he had several pairs of dentures. The last ones that he owned were made of hippopotamus ivory, gold, and brass.

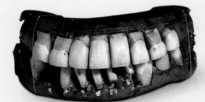

George Washington's false teeth

What did George Washington state about the slaves on his plantation in his will?

He stated that all of his slaves and their children were to be freed after his and his wife's deaths. He wrote that elderly slaves and those who were sick were to be cared for while they lived. The young were to be "taught to read and write."

Washington with two of his slaves

Timeline

A Hessian cap

On July 4, 1776, when representatives of the 13 British colonies signed the Declaration of Independence, it was far from certain that they could win that independence. But the Americans were determined to fight. When they defeated the British at the Battle of Saratoga in 1777, the tide began to turn. Still, it would be six more years before peace was reached and the new nation was free.

AUGUST 26, 1765 During the riots in Boston in protest over the Stamp Act, Lieutenant Governor Thomas Hutchinson's home is ransacked. The rioters steal his doors, furniture, silverware, and much more.

MARCH 5, 1770 A group of Patriots throws chunks of ice, oyster shells, and other items at British soldiers. The soldiers kill five people. The tragedy is named the Boston Massacre.

DECEMBER 16, 1773 The Boston Tea Party occurs when Patriots dress as Indigenous people, storm British ships, and throw their cargo of tea into Boston Harbor.

SEPTEMBER 5, 1774 After the port of Boston closes, delegates from all colonies, except Georgia, hold the First Continental Congress in Philadelphia to petition King George III formally to hear their grievances.

APRIL 18-19, 1775 Paul Revere tells John Hancock and Samuel Adams that British troops are planning to ambush the Patriots. He is captured after reaching Concord and later released.

APRIL 19, 1775 Colonial militiamen halt advancing British troops at the Battles of Lexington and Concord in Massachusetts, as the Revolutionary War begins.

JUNE 17, 1775 The British take heavy losses during the battles of Bunker Hill and Breed's Hill near Boston, but it allows them to take control of Charlestown Peninsula.

Montgomery's death at the Battle of Quebec

NOVEMBER–DECEMBER 1775 Patriots capture Montreal from British forces but are defeated at Quebec City on December 31. During the battle, Patriot commander Richard Montgomery is killed by cannon fire.

JANUARY 1, 1776 To celebrate the formation of the Continental Army, Washington flies the Grand Union flag near his Massachusetts headquarters.

JULY 4, 1776 Thomas Jefferson's draft of the Declaration of Independence is approved by the Second Continental Congress. Some delegates fear that it will unite Britain against them and lead to their destruction.

AUGUST 27, 1776 In the Battle of Long Island, the British and Hessian forces fight against the Continental Army, which is led by George Washington.

AUGUST 29-30, 1776 Washington's army evacuates Long Island and retreats to New York City.

Redcoats at Bunker Hill

SEPTEMBER 12, 1776 On Washington's orders, Patriot spy Nathan Hale goes to British-controlled Long Island disguised as a schoolmaster to look for intelligence about the movement of British troops.

SEPTEMBER 22, 1776 Hale is hanged after being captured by British soldiers.

JUNE 14, 1777 Congress declares that "the flag of the United States be made of thirteen stripes, alternate red and white; that the union be thirteen stars, white in a blue field, representing a new Constellation."

OCTOBER 4, 1777 At the Battle of Germantown, in Pennsylvania, Washington attacks British troops under Sir William Howe. The attack fails and he is forced to retreat. Howe is forced to resign after he spends the winter in Philadelphia instead of pursuing Patriots.

OCTOBER 7, 1777 General Burgoyne's British troops are defeated near Saratoga, New York.

OCTOBER 17, 1777 Burgoyne surrenders to General Gates.

DECEMBER 1777–MARCH 1778 The Continental Army spends a harsh winter at Valley Forge, Pennsylvania.

MAY 1778 Henry Clinton replaces Sir William Howe as commander of British troops in America.

Henry Clinton

DECEMBER 29, 1778 The British capture and occupy Savannah, Georgia.

FEBRUARY 25, 1779 On the Wabash River, General George Rogers Clark's troops capture Fort Vincennes from the British.

SEPTEMBER 23, 1780 Two days after General Benedict Arnold gives military secrets to British Major John André, André is captured, and Arnold flees to the British side.

OCTOBER 7, 1780 Americans defeat Scottish-led Loyalists at Kings Mountain, North Carolina.

JANUARY 17, 1781 Americans beat the British at Cowpens, South Carolina.

JANUARY 1781 Washington puts down rebellions by New Jersey and Pennsylvania regiments over lack of pay and low rations. However, they continue to fight the British.

MARCH 1, 1781 The Articles of Confederation go into effect in all 13 colonies.

MARCH 15, 1781 British general Lord Cornwallis defeats the colonists at Guilford Courthouse, North Carolina, then retreats to Yorktown, Virginia.

OCTOBER 19, 1781 At the Siege of Yorktown in Virginia, British commander Lord Cornwallis surrenders to George

A tin canteen used at the Battle of Germantown

Powder horn carried at Kings Mountain

Washington. Cornwallis sends his second-in-command to accept surrender.

APRIL 1, 1782 Washington settles his army near Newburgh, New York, to await the surrender of New York City.

NOVEMBER 30, 1782 The Treaty of Paris is drafted after months of negotiations.

SEPTEMBER 3, 1783 Britain and the US sign the Treaty of Paris, agreeing that all British troops will leave US territory and that US lands will extend to the Mississippi River in the west, and the Great Lakes and St. Lawrence River in the north, excluding the Spanish territories of Florida and West Florida in the south.

NOVEMBER 25, 1783 The last British soldiers leave New York.

DECEMBER 23, 1783 Washington returns his commander in chief's commission to Congress at Annapolis, Maryland, and returns to his home.

France's navy blockades Yorktown

Find out more

The American Revolution was fought throughout the original colonies, as well as in Ohio, Indiana, Florida, and even Canada. Visitors today can see the forts and battlefields where soldiers fought, and the weapons, uniforms, and personal possessions used during the war.

Guns of Fort Ticonderoga

During the 1775–1776 winter, Fort Ticonderoga's arsenal included more than 60 heavy cannon and mortars. Today, "Fort Ti" welcomes over 90,000 visitors each year, who can see one of the world's largest collections of 18th-century artillery.

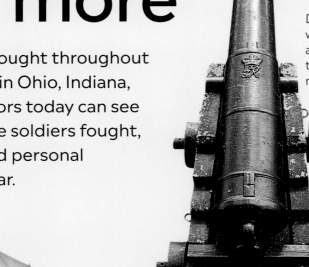

Cannon

Washington's writing desk

Birthplace of independence

Visitors can explore Independence Hall in Philadelphia. This was where the Declaration of Independence and the Constitution were signed.

Washington slept here

Visitors to the Colonial National Historical Park in Yorktown, Virginia, can see tents like this one used by George Washington at the Siege of Yorktown in 1781. Washington's Headquarters Tent during the Revolutionary War is on display at the Museum of the American Revolution in Philadelphia, Pennsylvania.

USEFUL WEBSITES

- The National Museum of American History has many items from Revolution-era America: **americanhistory.si.edu**
- The National Park Service's fact-filled site on the Revolution lets you tour places and view objects: **www.nps.gov/ subjects/americanrevolution/visit.htm**
- A companion website to the PBS series on the American Revolution: **www.pbs.org/ktca/liberty**
- A very thorough site with hundreds of helpful links: **www.americanrevolution.com**
- Learn about the Declaration of Independence at the National Archives: **www.archives.gov**

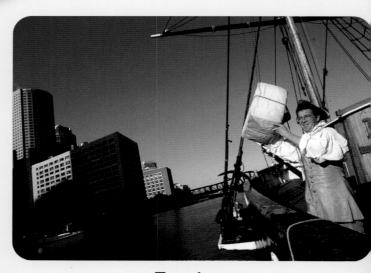

Tea time

Each year on December 16, performers dress as Indigenous people—some in elaborate Mohawk outfits—to reenact the Boston Tea Party of 1773. Visitors to the Boston Tea Party Ship and Museum in Boston Harbor can tour a life-sized replica of one of the ships and even hurl a bale of "tea" over the side of the boat.

History in art

This painting by Robert Wilson is on display at the Ninety Six Historical Site in South Carolina. Robert Wilson spent more than 500 hours researching and working on the painting. Before finishing it in 1977, he painted himself and his son into the action.

Artist Robert Wilson — — *Robert Wilson's son*

Patriots' Day

A Massachusetts state holiday commemorates the Battles of Lexington and Concord each year on April 19, when the first shots of the war were fired. A great place for your Patriots' Day celebration is Minuteman National Historic Park in Lexington and Concord, where families can watch actors in full costume honor that historic day.

PLACES TO VISIT

**MORRISTOWN NATIONAL HISTORICAL PARK
MORRISTOWN, NEW JERSEY**
This area was used twice as the Continental Army's winter encampment. It includes Washington's headquarters.

**COLONIAL WILLIAMSBURG
WILLIAMSBURG, VIRGINIA**
Colonial Williamsburg is the world's largest living history museum.

**MOORES CREEK NATIONAL BATTLEFIELD
CURRIE, NORTH CAROLINA**
Visit the site where the march of North Carolina Loyalists was stopped by Patriot cannon fire in February 1776.

**ADAMS NATIONAL HISTORICAL PARK
QUINCY, MASSACHUSETTS**
Don't miss the reenactment of the Declaration of Independence's historic passage at the home of five generations of Adamses, which included two presidents.

**ARKANSAS POST NATIONAL MEMORIAL
GILLETT, ARKANSAS**
The "Colbert Raid" in 1783 was the only Revolutionary War battle in Arkansas.

**INDIAN MILL STATE MEMORIAL
UPPER SANDUSKY, OHIO**
In June 1782, 500 Patriots battled British and the Delaware, Wyandot, Mingo, and Shawnee tribes here. A museum in an old gristmill is a highlight.

**FORT BOONESBOROUGH STATE PARK
RICHMOND, KENTUCKY**
In 1778, this fort bore a nine-day attack by Blackfish and his Shawnee tribe and Frenchmen.

Glossary

APOTHECARY A person, such as a pharmacist, who prepares and sells medicines and drugs.

APPRENTICE A person who learns a trade from another person.

ARTILLERY Mounted guns or the group of soldiers or branch of the military that use these weapons.

BARRACKS A building or buildings in a military garrison used to house soldiers.

Dragoon

BLACK POWDER An explosive powder made up of saltpeter, sulfur, and charcoal.

BLOCKADE The blocking of traffic, usually by sea, going into or out of a place, such as a seaport. Blockades were set up during war to prevent weapons and supplies from entering an enemy location.

BOMBARD To attack with artillery fire.

BOYCOTT An organized effort to stop using a certain kind of item, like English tea, to win a change in policy.

BUCKSKIN The skin of a buck, or male deer, often used for clothing.

CALIBER The diameter of a gun's interior barrel.

COURIER A messenger who carries diplomatic messages from one government to another.

DISCHARGE Official dismissal from active duty in the military.

DRAGOON In general, a member of a European cavalry in a heavily armed troop;

refers especially to a horse-mounted infantryman carrying a short musket.

ENCAMPMENT A camp or campsite.

ENLISTED MEN Men in the lower ranks of the military's chain of command, many of whom hold no commission or warrant.

FLOTILLA A group of small naval vessels containing two or more squadrons.

FORGE A special fireplace or furnace in which metal is heated by a blacksmith before it is shaped.

FORTIFICATION The act of fortifying or strengthening.

FUSILIER A soldier in the British army armed with fusils, a type of light flintlock musket.

GARRISON Troops stationed in a particular area, such as a fort, to defend it.

HOWITZER An artillery piece resembling a small cannon or large caliber gun with a short barrel.

INDIAN An earlier term used to refer to Indigenous Americans, the people who were native to the Americas and called it their home before the arrival of Europeans.

INDIGO A plant with red or purple flowers that are used to make blue dye; it was native in the Southern colonies.

LOOTING To carry off or steal.

LOUIS D'OR A French coin named after King Louis XIII; France stopped making them after the French Revolution.

LOYALIST (or TORY) A colonist who remained loyal to Great Britain and opposed the drive

for independence. About one-fifth of all citizens of the colonies were Loyalists.

MALARIA A deadly disease spread by mosquitoes.

MERCENARY A soldier who agrees to fight in a war for a foreign nation, usually in exchange for money or a share in the "spoils of war."

MILITIA A group of ordinary citizens not part of the regular army that is called into emergency military service.

MORTAR A type of cannon with a very short barrel but very wide bore, used for launching mortar shells at high angles.

MUSKET A smoothbore, single-shot, muzzle-loading shoulder gun. Infantrymen could fire three shots per minute from a flintlock musket. A long, triangular-shaped bayonet could be attached to the barrel to use as a weapon when the enemy was at arm's length.

MUSTER To assemble for battle, inspection, or roll call.

MUTINY An organized rebellion by a group of soldiers against the commanding officer or officers.

NEUTRAL Not taking sides, especially between two sides in a military conflict.

PARLIAMENT The national legislature of Great Britain, made up of the House of Commons and the House of Lords.

PATRIOT Those colonists during the Revolution who were active in fighting for independence.

PENCE The plural form of a British penny. Twelve pence equaled a shilling, and there were 20 shillings in a pound.

PETITION A written statement or plea, signed by a group of people that oppose a particular policy, requesting or demanding a change in that policy.

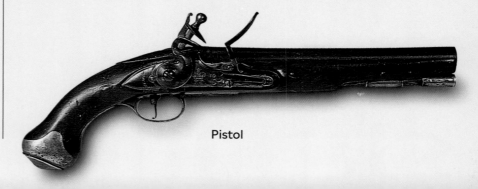

Pistol

Philipsburg Manor, a plantation in upstate New York

PILLAGE To strip of money or possessions by using violence, especially during war.

PISTOL A short gun that is designed to be aimed and fired with one hand.

PLANTATION A farm where crops such as cotton and rice are grown as cash crops and where the workforce lives on-site. During the American Revolution, the labor consisted of enslaved people forced to work without pay.

PROPAGANDA Information or ideas that are spread to others with the purpose of either promoting or hampering a cause.

PUBLIC HOUSE A tavern or inn, often used for political meetings during the Revolution.

REALES Silver Spanish coins that were worth one-eighth of a peso.

REINFORCEMENTS Additional troops or ships.

REGIMENT A military unit made up of two or more smaller battle groups called battalions, as well as a headquarters group and other supporting groups.

SABER A heavy sword with one sharp edge, usually curved, that was used by cavalrymen.

SHARPSHOOTER A person who shoots a gun with especially good aim.

A jacket button for a South Carolina regiment

"SC 3" markings for South Carolina, 3rd Regiment

SIEGE A military maneuver in which one force surrounds or blockades a fortification so that supplies will be cut off from the outside, in the hope of leading to a surrender.

SMALLPOX A deadly and highly contagious disease that causes fever and skin blisters.

SMOOTHBORE Refers to a gun with a smooth bore (inside barrel surface).

SOAPSTONE A soft mineral that has a soapy feel, used as material for bullet molds, fireplaces, and sinks.

SQUADRONS A group of two or more divisions of a fleet of ships.

SURVEYOR A person who takes exact measurements to determine the boundaries, area, and elevation of a certain piece of land.

Saber

THEORIST A person who deals with concepts or explanations behind an idea.

TOMAHAWK A small ax used by Indigenous warriors as a weapon or tool.

TRICORN A popular Revolution-era hat, in which the brim is turned up on three sides to form corners.

TURNCOAT A traitor.

TYPHUS A deadly disease caused by bacteria and spread by lice, fleas, or ticks; common in the crowded and unclean encampments of the Revolutionary War.

Union Jack

UNION JACK A popular term for the national flag of Great Britain. It is made up of a red and white cross representing England, a diagonal white cross representing Scotland, and a diagonal red cross representing Ireland.

VOLUNTEER A person who offers his or her service freely.

Index

Acknowledgments

The publisher would like to thank the following people for their help with making the book: Catherine H. Grosfils, Colonial Williamsburg Foundation; Christopher D. Fox, Fort Ticonderoga Museum; Joan Bacharach and Khaled Bassim, National Park Service, Museum Management Program; Carol Haines, Concord Museum (www.concordmuseum.org); Peter Harrington, Anne S. K. Brown Military Collection; Richard Malley, Connecticut Historical Society; Andrea Ashby, Independence National Historical Park; Claudia Jew, The Mariners' Museum; and Tordis Isselhardt, Images from the Past; Ashwin Khurana for editorial assistance; Ashok Kumar for DTP assistance; Saloni Singh and Priyanka Sharma-Saddi for the jacket; Vagisha Pushp for picture research; Bianca Hezekiah for the authenticity review; Lisa Eyre for proofreading; and Helen Iddles for the index.

Smithsonian's National Museum of American History: :
Jennifer L. Jones, Curator, Military History
Kathy Golden, Curator, Military History
David D. Miller III, Curator, Military History

Smithsonian Enterprises:

Kealy Gordon, Product Development Manager
Jill Corcoran, Director, Licensed Publishing
Brigid Ferraro, Vice President, Business Development and Licensing
Carol LeBlanc, President

The publisher would like to thank the following for their kind permission to reproduce their images:

(Key: t = top; b = bottom; l = left; r = right; c = center)

Alamy Stock Photo: Paul Kim 7br; Niday Picture Library 11tr; The Granger Collection 13br; Reuters / Jim Urquhart 15br; Historic Images 29tc; Ian Dagnall 29b; Artokoloro 34br; North Wind Picture Archives 36br, 49br, 59tr; Granger Historical Picture Archive, NYC 44tl, 56cra; Science History Images / Photo

Researchers 51t; The Picture Art Collection 54bc; incamerastock / ICP 61tl. **Abby Aldrich Rockefeller Folk Art Museum, Williamsburg, VA:** 7tr, 39bl. *The American Revolution*, by John Fiske: 8crb, 12cl, 13bl, 18cr, 28cl, 31tr, 41br, 42c, 44bl, 46tr, 47bc, 47br, 56bl, 56cr, 57bl, 58tr, 59cr. **Anne S.K. Brown Military Collection, Brown University Library:** 12bl, 17t, 18-19t, 19b, 27b. **Boston Tea Party Chapter, DAR:** 11c. **Bridgeman Images:** © Don Troiani 4bl, 23tr; © Philadelphia Museum of Art / Gift of Dorothea Wood, 1959 41tl, 49bc; © Boltin Picture Library 38r; © **David Cain:** 8tr, 24tr. **Center of Military History, H. Charles McBarron:** 24bl, 31b, 32b, 35b, 55br, 57t, 59br. **The Colonel Charles Waterhouse Historical Museum:** 20b, 25b, 41t. **Colonial Williamsburg Foundation:** 7c, 10c, 12br, 12tr, 14cl, 15c, 23bl, 46cr, 48c, 49crb, 51br, 53tr, 61bc. **Concord Museum, Concord, Massachusetts:** 16tc, 39c, 59c, 61tr. **Connecticut Historical Society:** 16bl, 16cl, 19cl, 19tr, 24c, 46tl, 48b, 51ca, 58fcl, 59tl. **Dahl Taylor:** 6tl. © **David R. Wagner, 1994:** 64b. **Delaware Art Museum:** 66b. Painting by Don Troiani, www.historicalartprints.com: 70tl. **Photos courtesy of Don Troiani, www.historicalartprints. com:** 66tl, 67tr, 67tl, 70b, 71c, 71bl. **Dover Publications:** 15tl, 21tr, 31tl, 34tl, 42bc, 44cl, 46bl. **Dreamstime.com:** F11photo 39tr; William Perry 40cla; **Fort Ticonderoga Museum:** 4tr, 9c, 9cr, 15tc, 17bl, 17br, 17tr, 19c, 22c, 22tr, 46c, 68tr. © **The Frick Collection, New York:** 32cl. **Getty Images:** Bettmann 14bl, Popperfoto 28tr. **Photo courtesy of Ian Britton:** 69b; **Independence National Historical Park:** 13cl, 13crb, 21cr, 27cla, 27bl, 31cl, 36tr, 52tr, 55bl, 68cr. **The Institute of Heraldry:** 59bl (drawing by James Burmester). **James Burmester:** 66; **Library of Congress:** 7cla (State House), 8cl, 8tr, 9c, 10b, 11b, 11cra, 12bc, 14bl, 15bc, 15bl, 18b, 19tc, 22b, 23tl, 24br, 26br, 27cr, 29tl, 33cl, 34tr, 35clb, 36cl, 39cbl, 39tl, 40br, 42bl, 42br, 42tr, 45b, 45cr, 45tr, 47t, 53tl, 55t, 58b, 61br, 61cb, 62br, 63cr, 65br, 67bl, 67br. **Lexington, Massachusetts Historical Society:** 17c, 17cl. **Marblehead Historical Society, Marblehead, MA:** 6cb. **The Mariners' Museum, Newport News, VA:** 9t, 38cl, 43t, 43br, 36cb. **Massachusetts Historical Society:** lOcr. **Morristown National Historical Park:** 44br. **Mount Vernon Ladies' Association:** 13tl, 65c, 65cr. **MPI Archives:** 7tl (banknote), 40bl, 63cl. **National**

Archives: 16tl, 58c, 60cra. **National Museum of American History:** 6bl, 6br, 9cl, 10cl, 21bl, 25c, 25t, 26c, 29c, 39br, 63bc, 63br, 64tr, 68cl. **National Numismatics Collection:** 40cb, 40ct, 43bc, 43bl, 50cl, 50fcl. **National Park Service:** 21cl, 21br, 31c, 37tr, 37b, 37tc, 53cr. **National Park Service, Don Troiani:** 20tl, 22cr, 22tl, 23br, 23tc, 35tr, 37tl, 50br, 52-53b, 54c, 54br. **National Park Service, Museum Management Program and Guilford Courthouse National Military Park, photos by Khaled Bassim:** 29crb, 29cr, 41c, 45c, 45cl, 45tc, 45tl, 48tl, 49tc (corkscrew), 49t (pipe), 49ca, 49cra, 50tr, 51bc, 51bl, 52crb, 52cr, 53crb, 53br, 53cb, 55crb, 55cb, 57cr, 58cl (lead bullets). **National Park Service, Museum Management Program and Valley Forge National Historical Park, photos by Carol Highsmith and Khaled Bassim:** 9bl, 14br, 14crb, 15tr, 21bc, 21tr, 23c, 23clb, 23cl, 30r, 31cr, 33tc, 33tl, 35cr, 36bl, 36tl, 37cr, 41tr, 47bl, 51tr, 51crt, 54cl, 56cl, 57bc. **National Portrait Gallery:** 11tl, 13c, 14tl, 26tr, 33tr, 35ca, 41bl, 44cr, 46br, 50tl, 61cr, 63bl, 64tl. **Peter Newark's Pictures:** 26bl. © **Robert Holmes/CORBIS:** 68br. **Painting courtesy of Robert Wilson, Jr.:** 69cla; © **Ron Toelke Associates:** 30l, 32tr, 54tl. **Smithsonian American Art Museum:** 16br, 23cra. **Sons of the Cincinnati:** 65cla. **Sons of the Revolution in the State of New York, Inc./ Fraunces Tavern® Museum, New York City:** 31br, 62bl. **State Historical Society of Wisconsin:** 8bl. **SuperStock:** 18cb. **U.S. Capitol:** 27t, 33br, 57br, 63t. **U.S. Department of Defense:** The appearance of U.S. Department of Defense (DoD) visual information does not imply or constitute DoD endorsement 4crb, 59bc. **U.S. Senate Collection:** 28b, 62tr. ©**1996, Virginia Historical Society, Lora Robins Collection of Virginia Art:** 13tr. **West Point Museum, Photos © Paul Warchol Photography, Inc.:** 24cr, 33cr, 33bl, 62cl. **Winterthur Museum:** 60b.

All other images © Dorling Kindersley
For further information see:
www.dkimages.com